W9-AJQ-088

808
LO

Lowery, Marilyn M.

How to write romance
novels that sell

How to Write Romance Novels That Sell

MARILYN M. LOWERY

Rawson Associates

NEW YORK

Library of Congress Cataloging in Publication Data
Lowery, Marilyn M.
  How to write romance novels that sell.

  Bibliography: p.
  Includes index.
  1. Love stories—Authorship. I. Title.
PN3377.5.L68L69   1983   808'.02   82-24052
ISBN 0-89256-224-2
ISBN 0-89256-239-0 (pbk.)

Composition by P & M Typesetting, Inc., Waterbury, Conn.
Manufactured by Fairfield Graphics, Fairfield, Pennsylvania
Designed by Kathleen Carey
First Edition

For my students in Writing the Romance

"... *your* defect is a propensity to hate everybody."

"And yours," he replied with a smile, "is wilfully to misunderstand them."

JANE AUSTEN, *Pride and Prejudice*

Contents

Introduction: Before You Read This Book

I first became interested in writing the romance when I was teaching English literature to high school honors students and encouraging them not to waste their time on paperback romances. Over the months, no one paid attention to me. I observed, especially, one girl who read at least three of these novels a day. As I watched her slim down, become more graceful, more stylish, and less shy, it appeared that she was identifying with these heroines, that they were making a genuine contribution to her well-being. The school library was having a sale, so I bought most of the popular romances, read them, and decided to contribute to this form myself as Philippa Castle.

Successful category fiction relies on techniques that can be learned: creating the exciting hero and heroine, bringing them to life with believable dialogue, creating suspense with twists of plot, setting the two in an exotic ambiance, paralleling or contrasting their situation with supporting characters, and, throughout, conjuring the true romantic mood. For it is romance, more than overt sex, that the readers desire.

Romances are now available for every taste. Publishers' demographics show that a majority of romance readers fall between the ages of twenty-six and thirty-six and have careers, so publishers are presenting books in which the heroine is older and less helpless than were previous heroines. She is no longer the secretary—she is the boss. She is unashamedly sensual and permits herself to indulge in sex, but an aura of romance still pervades the story.

There are historical romances for readers who like longer stories with more adventure and sex; period romances such as the Regencies or Georgians for those who like love relationships as they were in centuries past, and contemporary romances for those who want to identify with the modern heroine. Romances for the young adult have a heroine and hero of the appropriate age. One type of romance is written for homosexuals; another, for various ethnic groups. A romance novel exists for every reader.

For centuries, only men wrote romances. Even the Brontë sisters first published under men's names. Now the genre is dominated by women writers. Though men are not excluded, only a small number write for the romance market, and usually under women's pseudonyms.

My purpose in writing this book is to help you write the types of books romance editors buy. You will read romances that don't follow the formula. Listed below are some of the reasons why novels in print do not always reflect the editor's requirements:

1. Sometimes editors must buy a certain number of books in a hurry and take anything at hand.

2. To compete favorably on the market, editors attempt new approaches and may just as quickly drop them.

3. An editor might have bought too many books with a similar plot line and may decide that particular approach has been overworked.

4. Editors change houses frequently, and a new editor might call for plot changes.

5. Most important, a book might be so well written that any change in the formula can be overlooked.

Under the various categories, I have not only pointed out the rule but have given some exceptions to the rule.

In the following pages, I refer to the classics of romantic literature to show you leading works that helped to determine the formula. I also take examples from popular romances, demonstrating ways to approach specific writing problems. The examples I use are not based upon an author's popularity, but upon the appropriateness of the passage itself.

Most good stories are in some sense love stories. The very first novel in the English language, Samuel Richardson's eighteenth-century *Pamela,* was a romance. The popular romance looks to the best in our literature and is blossoming today in myriad forms to delight the modern reader. The key ingredient is the perfect love; and the key to creating this love and making it believable lies in the craft that you, too, can practice.

I

Romance Writers as Heroines

SUCCESS. It is a universal dream that eludes most people; yet like the romance heroines who plunge into adventures and find themselves facing formidable odds, many women take the risks, write the stories they have longed to share, and do succeed in the publishing world. Today, romances are flourishing as never before, and those women who have the strength of character to be willing to set down their thoughts, to be vulnerable to a vast audience of readers, are finding glass slippers that fit and coaches that whisk them to the rewarding world of the writer.

I have spoken to some writers who have taken this journey and have earned some monetary reward. However, to them, success and reward also mean doing what they love to do, and sharing with an appreciative audience. What all the writers here have in common is that they had to struggle to do their writing. They had to overcome the demands of small children or demanding jobs or even illness.

Nevertheless, they learned to make compromises or adjustments in order to steal writing time. They all had a dream, and they wrote that dream.

You, too, may read romances, and you may know that you could write them if only there were not so many hindrances in your life. None of the writers interviewed had an easy time; but eventually they did sell. Perhaps their true-life stories will encourage you to work to join them.

Haunted by Dreams

LaVyrle Spencer dreamed her first novel, *The Fulfillment* (Avon). "I dreamed my plot, time and time again for two years—literally, at night—nighttime dreamed it. I would wake up and couldn't go back to sleep because I'd be so excited about it. It would be very clear. The setting was my grandmother's farm that I used to stay at when I was a child. Many of the events were things that I had either experienced or had heard my parents or my grandparents talk about; and it was vivid. So I began the book at four in the morning one time when the dream woke me again. I said to myself, 'If this story wants to get written, then it's time to get out of bed and start writing.' All I had to work with, at that time, was a pencil and a notebook and a dictionary. And that's the way I started. I knew nothing."

What led Spencer to romance writing? "I have never been to college, but I studied writing in a sophomore English class in high school. The teacher encouraged me; and the idea that I could be a professional writer lay dormant in my mind for years, until I read Kathleen E. Woodiwiss's *The Flame and the Flower* (Avon). I studied it like a Bible. I began fantasizing about meeting Kathleen Woodiwiss and writing something that would do for others the sort of thing her book had done for me."

Spencer used to lie in bed at night and wonder, What

makes me love a romance? Her answer: "When a man and a woman are allowed to make love together, and they deny themselves. Put them in the same building. Don't put them across town from each other or in two different cities." Spencer sees the lovers in a situation in which not distance but their own consciences keep them apart.

The path was not easy for her. She was working nine months of the year as an aide in the media department at a local junior high school. She had two daughters who were in junior high school at that time, 1976. "We did have conflicts here during those two summers that I really isolated myself because this was a thing I just had to do. I couldn't *not* do it. They were jealous of the time that I closed myself away and said to them, 'Turn down the stereo,' 'Don't bother me unless it's an emergency.' I closed myself in my bedroom and wrote, wrote, wrote."

Spencer first met Woodiwiss at a local bookstore. "Earlier I had typed a long letter telling her how she had inspired me. When I stepped up in front of her, I was so choked up I could hardly talk. I shook her hand, gave my name, and said, 'You can't know what it means for me to meet you.' I was crying and had my hands over my mouth and I was saying, 'Oh, my God!' I thrust my letter into her hands and said, 'Take this and read it.' I hightailed it out of there, got to my car, and discovered I'd forgotten to take a picture. I thought, 'Do I dare go back?' Well, I did, and we talked. She was very gracious and answered my questions about how to type a manuscript. I was still longhanding it."

When Spencer first finished her manuscript, after two summers of work, she was not quite satisfied with it, but her summer writing time was up. She sent it to Avon, Woodiwiss's publisher, and it was rejected. Undaunted, she rewrote it. This time she called Woodiwiss. "I took a big gulp, called her up, and asked if she would read it. She said yes, and it was sent right out of her house to Avon in New York, where it was accepted."

Spencer suffered two rejections from Avon after her first

sale. "Selling my book to the only house that ever read it and then having that house reject me afterwards—they gave me my start, and then broke my heart. I pulled out of it, but those days after the second rejection were perhaps the lowest of my writing life. I just about did stop writing. I was already looking at ads in the paper, deciding that I would go out and get a job as a secretary because I could not hack it emotionally. I just almost buckled under the rejections."

Spencer then sent her second manuscript, *The Endearment,* to Richard Gallen Books, where it was accepted. Her name was made by those first two books. "I'm not convinced I'm a success. I always thought success meant sales, and I haven't had a whole lot of sales yet. My first print run [number of books printed] for *The Fulfillment* was 114,000 and for *The Endearment,* 110,000. But I do get a lot of authors who write to me and say they study my books."

To overcome a writer's block she recently suffered and to make money after her husband was laid off, Spencer signed to do the shorter Second Chance at Love series. Changing to a different type of romance has helped her out of her block, but she exclaims, "It's hard! What's easy is that you don't have to dig, dig for every fact about everyday life as you do with historicals; but you do have to research and be accurate in your facts, more so for today than in the past because if you ever use an improper term, the readers will know it. You still have to develop your story, but you have less time to do it. And you'd better do it craftily, and your dialogue has to be so *crisp*. I found that good dialogue is the most important thing in the small romance. Also, I think it's very difficult to come up with a fresh way of describing the hero and heroine without the narrator taking over. So imagination has to really work, and innovation, and that's not easy."

Spencer doesn't write a specific number of words a day. "There is virtually not a day that goes by that I do not devote to my career; but that does include being my own secretary, which is very time-consuming."

What gives Spencer's books appeal? First, she plans her story well. In *The Fulfillment,* she outlined the events in the span of a year. "My whole plot parallels one season of farming: planting the seed, watching it grow, nurturing it, reaping the harvest, and taking it in—symbolizing what was happening to the woman." Spencer went to her grandmother's farm, made tapes, then put the information onto a graph, month by month. "That became the day-to-day life of my characters. I already knew the love story— what caused the rift and who would end up together—all that was in the dream."

Second, she believes in making her scenes real for the reader. "I think when you are writing a romance, it is very important that you tell the reader precisely every body motion, particularly in a love scene. It just isn't enough to tell the reader, 'He brought her to the height of ecstasy.' " Spencer complains that the majority of romances euphemize a love scene until we no longer know what the body movements are. "Also, if there's a very tense moment, where in the room is the man standing? Where is the woman standing? What is she thinking? What is she looking at? Is she staring at the knob on the front of the old wood stove? Is she thinking about the fire? All of these things are what the reader wants to hear."

Third, Spencer appeals to the five senses. "Countless authors never realize that when they're responding to a book that they love, it's because all five senses have been brought into play."

Her advice to new writers is to analyze and take notes. "When I come across something I love, I write it down in a little notebook. I go back to it and pull it out and read it." She also believes in taking a positive attitude. She advises would-be writers not to be scared away from writing, thinking it is too difficult to get published. She tells them, "Give writing a try."

Her own work can best be summarized by the three goals she keeps in mind. "I try to make my readers laugh, to make them cry, and to make them respond sexually. If I do all three to the reader, then I give myself as many stars as you can give. If I do two, okay. If I do only one, then I'd better work a little harder."

Reordering Priorities

Celeste De Blasis had always planned to be a writer, but on the side. "It was going to be a hobby. Not that I wanted it to be, but you couldn't make a living being a writer. Even though I hadn't been totally conventional, there was a part of me that, like most good little girls, was raised to please a lot of other people before I pleased myself."

Then she discovered after college that she had lupus, an incurable disease of the immune system, causing the body to react to the ultraviolet light of the sun and to stress. "I discovered I could live a very long time with it or I might die of it a lot sooner than I had planned. It really reordered my priorities. I suddenly thought, I don't have time to do with my life what everyone else wants me to do with it—I'm going to have to use the time very wisely. There's a great peace in that."

Was getting started difficult? "A friend of mine at Universal Studios read some of my prose, liked it, and said, 'I think it's good enough to have a good agent.' He gave me an introduction to a Los Angeles agent who was going to be away for eight months. He, in turn, referred me to a New York agent." These first prose works were a mystery and a short story. The New York agent suggested that De Blasis do a hardcover novel.

She was still doing a lot of jobs she didn't like but that supported her "more or less," so she could write and paint. Yet another tragedy acted as a spur to her writing. A brother, David, two years younger, came home from overseas in 1971 with incurable cancer. As he lay dying, De Blasis's verse became "totally obsessed with death. It was sort of like my own victory over not caring about the quantity of life." She found, however, that though it is possible to sustain that feeling about your own existence, it isn't easy to sustain the feeling for someone you love.

With the agent's encouragement, she wrote a Gothic novel, *The Night Child* (Coward, McCann & Geoghegan), finishing the manuscript one week before David died. "Some kind of adversity had a lot to do with redirecting my energies." She adds, "There's so much power in being in a novel. It really kept me sane when David was dying to be writing *The Night Child* because even though characters begin to take on a life of their own—and they live totally separate from you if they're good characters—at the same time, it is a totally controlled world where you know what's happening. That can be wonderful when the rest of the world is falling apart. I think novelists discover that. There's enormous enchantment in the work."

What about this first book appealed to the editor and resulted in a sale? "The characters were very appealing; and despite the Gothic structure, they were very real. Also, it had a twist to it, not knowing whether the child was good or evil. The editor liked the prose style, so there were very few changes."

Another clue to De Blasis's appeal comes from her comment about another novel of hers, *The Tiger's Woman* (Delacorte). "The people on the island seem totally real to me. . . . All the people there had sustained some kind of terrible pain in the outside world, and the isolation was something they sought rather than its being a burden to them. Their acceptance of each other was complete because they saw beyond the exterior things. I think that generates a kind of warmth that people are willing to respond to."

She had good luck with her second book, a romantic suspense novel, and thinks her agent had a lot to do with that. "Sometimes I feel I got on a fast bus. I started writing in '71; from '72 to '73 I wrote *The Night Child*. Now I'm on my fifth book." Since that second book, she has written historical novels.

How many books did she have to write to establish her reputation? "It takes several books. The appeal was there and the audience was there from the beginning, but *The Proud Breed* (Coward, McCann & Geoghegan) was the first book to come out in numbers. The Doubleday Book Club sold nearly half a million copies and the Fawcett paperback edition sold six hundred thousand, so the readership is over one million."

How many words a day does she aim for? "Sometimes I'll go for a word count to get something structured. If the writing's going well, I'll work right through. Some days it's only two paragraphs. How long a work takes depends on how the writing is going and on how difficult the passages are."

What would she tell new writers? "Writing is a craft like anything else. It is not this dreamy thing where someone says, 'I love your book. I'm going to publish it all over the world.' New writers can't conceive of the fact that it's something you serve an apprenticeship in, just like any other profession.

"I studied literature. I had this theory that nobody can make a writer, that you're either born with that or you're not. But what you need to do is to know an awful lot about what has already been written. If you just read, read, read and study literature, you'll at least have an idea of what not to do again. A lot of times writing teachers, at least in my college experience, are really disappointed writers, and they have a lot of bitterness and venom to offer their students."

A final bit of advice is *to observe*. "It's taken me a long time to be aware of this. I test every single day: How does it feel? How does it look? If you don't have that skill, you can train yourself to do it. Stop and use all your senses. On a day like this, the heat can make animals do strange things. Birds outside my window are fluttering nervously and coming in low because it's going to rain. My grandmother started me in birding when I was very small, and she also knew all the plants. Once you're trained this way, it's a lot harder to do damage to the world."

De Blasis concludes, "One of the senses I have is that

time really is precious. One of the characteristics of lupus is that a lot of times, when it's active, you feel so tired that it's very difficult to do anything; so I think that motivation is important, that you have to do it right then. Nothing makes me angrier than someone who comes up and says casually, 'Oh, yes, I'm going to write a book someday, as soon as I have time.' "

Age No Barrier

Violet Ashton, born in 1908, says, "I think Barbara Cartland and I are the two oldest romance writers writing. All her heroines are virgins, and mine are anything but." Ashton did not sell her first novel until 1976, when she was sixty-eight, but she always wrote, mostly poetry.

Though on her mother's side Ashton stems from a long line of writers, including Jonathan Swift, the eighteenth-century satirist, her own life was "one of hard work and a Depression and of trying to rear three little children born in the heart of the Depression." Her first marriage was "one of those romances that soon die in a Depression. It was a dreadful time." Ashton managed by writing, mostly verse, when the children were in bed or in school. She has had many small pieces published in newspapers. "Then I went to work and had to write only at night. I did a very menial job. I worked in a doughnut shop. I wasn't qualified for anything. All I ever wanted to do was write."

Ashton explains that her first book, *Delphine,* was actually written in the mid-forties. "I threw it out once in the garbage can, then ran and got it just two steps ahead of the garbage collector." In 1974 she joined Writers' Workshop West in Los Angeles, "a very encouraging group." In 1976 she was inspired to send *Delphine* to a New York agent. A few months later, it was sold to Fawcett as *Love's Triumphant Heart,* and has been published in the United States, England, Australia, New Zealand, and Norway.

Did she have an agent to help with all sales? "Yes. I looked in *Writer's Market* and liked a particular name. His write-up wasn't ostentatious. He's English; and being a Canadian, I liked that very much. I got him immediately, and he has sold all my books."

What led her to write a historical novel? "I am self-educated. I grew up on tales of the history of my own family, and books were our TV. We read history and historical novels. Ours was one of the few homesteads in that arid plain [Saskatchewan, Canada] that had books. We had such contented childhoods, reading those long, long winters, clustered 'round the oak table, the coal oil lamps . . . they're wonderful memories." Why did she use the romance form? "I loved romance. I'd have been very happy to have been born into the era of candlelight and the French minuet. I thought I was the romantic person from about fourteen on. I read *Dracula* when I was nine, and I used to spend a lot of time under beds. Oh, I think I fell in love with that bloodthirsty count who to me was—there's the romance coming in, you see—to me, always, he was an evil but *fascinating* man."

After she sold her first romance, which takes place in the Napoleonic era, she was able to devote herself to writing, and she sold three more in rapid succession. The second was a sequel called *Love's Rebellious Pleasure* (Fawcett). She then chose prerevolutionary Russia as the setting for her next two books. "At my late date, I suppose I'd been all pent up. I'm a rapid writer anyway, so I sold one book a year."

Ashton doesn't have a writing schedule. "I write until I'm written out. It doesn't matter if it's hours. If it isn't going well, I'll shut it out and do something else. Otherwise, I'll write until I'm satisfied with what I've done. Then I just automatically stop. I have gone for eight or nine or ten hours. The natural stop seems to come to me."

What distinguishes her works and gives her a hearing? "I've had several people pick out the same things in my books. Perhaps I have the ability to make people feel. Fans have said they feel emotionally drained after reading one of my books."

How many books did she sell before becoming known? "I don't feel especially well known, but my novels have gone fairly well. I have about eighteen scrapbooks about them, including fan letters."

Ashton tells new writers, "Persevere. If you love writing, don't let anybody destroy your dream. Of course, the ultimate triumph is when you sell; but just to take great joy in what you write, that's important."

She concludes, "I don't fight a dry spell. It's like so many of those prairie wells my poor dad used to dig. It's dry and the water won't come in. And the word won't come in until it's ready. I can't sit down at my typewriter and force myself to write because what I turn out is no good. Once I get an idea, I'm off and running, but that idea has to come. That idea usually has to have something emotional in it for me. I'm moved by something that happens, and I am almost every day of my life—in the papers, one way or another. I can very easily write something concerning it."

Selling, a Slow Process

Patricia Matthews, often called America's first lady of historical romance, has been writing for twenty-five years. "Like many novelists, I started small with poetry. My first story sales were to men's magazines, which bought science fiction." With two young children from her first marriage, it wasn't easy for Matthews to find writing time. "Sales were few and far between—just enough to keep me going."

After her divorce from her first husband, in 1961, Matthews took a job with California State University, Los Angeles, where she worked for seventeen years, first in the accounting department and later as office manager for the Associated Students' office. Writing had to be relegated to evening hours, mostly after the children were in bed. "Luckily, I can work with a fair amount of distraction, and I can be interrupted and go back to work. I'm very adaptable and flexible. I could write on weekends when the kids were coming in and out."

When getting started, Matthews took a class at Mount San Antonio College. "A class gives the new writer the courage to put her thoughts down on paper and teaches the technical things a writer needs to know." A writers' group that still meets and shares material grew out of that class.

Sales were very gradual, and it was many years before she became one of the leading ladies of romance. "Most of us spent a lot of time and wrote lots and lots of things before anything got accepted." She confesses, "I have my little trunk of rejection slips like everyone else."

In 1976, at the suggestion of her agent, she wrote a historical romance, *Love's Avenging Heart* (Pinnacle). Soon it was on the best-seller list, and Matthews was established as a leading romance writer. A ten-book series, with *love* in the title of each book, followed.

What led to Matthews's remarkable success? First, she spent time learning and polishing her craft. "I wrote poetry, short stories, juveniles, and Gothics." Second, she approached her stories with feeling. "You must write from the heart. I try to make the characters as real as possible. The story is melodramatic in a sense, larger than life; so I try to keep the characters believable." Third, she is never condescending. "I try not to cheat the reader. I give it my best shot." Fourth, she gives a broad sweep, a true feeling of adventure. "I like a story to be romantic in the broad sense. I like mystery." And fifth, she tries to avoid a rigid formula, which she calls "a bane to creativity." Until she was established, Matthews stayed close to what the writers who had popularized the historical romance were doing. "With each successive novel, I tried to get farther away from that pattern without losing the audience."

Where does she get her ideas? "I use what I know of psychology and other people's fantasies. Unlike some romance writers, I don't draw from my own fantasies." Setting helps to spark ideas for her. She picked Williamsburg, Virginia, for the background in *Love's Avenging Heart* because she had traveled there and it had piqued her imagination. She spends part of every year traveling to and doing research at the actual site of her next book. "Excitement, mystery, and emotion are the three main ingredients in every one of my stories; however, I attempt to make each story different from the others. The reader is getting more sophisticated. Once you're offered a plethora of choices, you get choosier and you get tired of the same thing."

What advice would she give beginning authors? "By and large, if you really want to write and you really have reason to think you have some talent, you have to be willing to stay with it and be prepared to work hard. I think most people who write don't do it principally for the money; and the number of those who make a success in any of the arts is very small. They do it mostly for love. It's a rough and a very competitive field, so I think you have to care about it and have to be willing to spend some time.

"Take a writing class at your local college or high school," she encourages new writers. "At a certain stage of your development, you need to learn the rudiments and to get over your initial embarrassment."

Matthews stresses the need for a writer to be dedicated and to be consistent in her work. Though she now writes about two thousand words a day, on a word processor, for years she didn't write much at a time, but she did it consistently. "I saw a lot of people with talent fall by the wayside just because they didn't keep on writing."

Repeated Rejections

When new Harlequin author Alison Quinn talks about writing, she says, "I struggled all my life." She had many near successes with stories and plays, with requests by editors for more. She would write the requested work, and it would be rejected. This pattern continued for a number of years. A *Woman's Home Companion* editor told her, "Your stories are charming, your technique is wonderful. When you hit a topic that is typical of us . . ." Quinn says, "I guess I never did. I always had to do something different."

Quinn had odd hours when she taught dancing and drama at the Loretta Young Studio, so she wrote in between working hours. Later, when she worked for the John Robert Powers Studio, teaching personal development (including drama, speech, etiquette, and the art of dress), she wrote at night. Eventually, she took her course to Pasadena City College and while there, took a course in writing for publication. "I got a lot out of the course. I wrote my first book, *The Satyr Ring* (Harlequin), while I was going to class, and read it to the group chapter by chapter. I had never written a book, but suddenly I just knew how to do it. Of course, I had written plays. The class confirmed what I did, kept my confidence going."

How did she get the idea for her book? "Once I met a melancholy man who had an enormous, strange ring with the face of a satyr. Years later a story came over me. I mulled it over before putting it down. At first it was about the man with the ring, but I changed the character to a woman. I don't recall what he had said, and he has no relation to my story, but he did inspire me."

Quinn had no trouble selling the Gothic to Harlequin Books, where she first sent it; and they have asked for a second. Quinn thinks its appeal is that it has a strong story line with mystery and a great deal of conflict. Harlequin's 1983 line of Gothics has been tested in plain covers on readers throughout the country, and *The Satyr Ring* has received the top rating. What else besides a good story helped to get Quinn this rating? "The rhythms. I have a feel for language. I love poetry. Reading it helps me write better prose. I like to write with a lot of feeling. My scenes have a lot of emotion in them."

Quinn writes each morning from nine to noon. "I used to be a night person, but found I write best in the morning. I go for ideas, not numbers of words or pages, so I have no idea how much I write a day. I do like to stop a scene in the middle, when I know how it will end. That way, I can get started quickly the next morning."

Quinn suggests that new writers use good taste in sex scenes. "I am against rape scenes. We have so much on the downbeat. Feeding people violence—I could never do it. Rape is a double violence to me; it violates love as well as the physical body. The sensitivity and the mystery are taken out of life if you go into the sexually explicit. In my books, every love scene has a real background and purpose."

Quinn also advises new writers to "keep at it, steadily, steadily. I could have given up, I had so many heartbreaks. But I just couldn't stop. I held on. Being on the edge of a sale is almost more heartbreaking than not having any attention at all. It was really very painful, but I did keep on. You never know when you're on the edge of really getting something, so it's worth hanging on. Maybe you will make it."

Your Own Adventure

All the romance writers interviewed are voracious readers. Some are college educated; others are self-educated through books. They all struggled to get where they are. Now they enjoy contributing to that fantasy world from which they have gained so much.

It is a world to which you, too, may want to contribute. These authors have shared their stories to give you encouragement. If your typewriter is broken or you don't own one, pick up a pen or pencil. If no one believes in you, believe in yourself. These writers did not wait for someone else's prodding. If you have writing talent, you will find that a great satisfaction comes from fulfillment.

Celeste De Blasis reminds us, "Time is precious." If you long to write, today is the day to start your own adventure. It isn't easy. It takes spunk. But if you are determined, you can join the heroines in the world of romance.

II

Getting Started

The Traditional Romance Formula

ROMANCES are based on a traditional formula, which has many variations:

1. A girl, our heroine, meets a man, our hero, who is above her socially and who is wealthy and worldly.

2. The hero excites the heroine but frightens her sexually.

3. She is usually alone in the world and vulnerable.

4. The hero dominates the heroine, but she is fiery and sensual, needing this powerful male.

5. Though appearing to scorn her, the hero is intrigued by her and pursues her sexually.

6. The heroine wants love, not merely sex, and sees his pursuit as self-gratification.

7. The two clash in verbal sparring.

8. In holding to her own standards, the heroine appears to lose the hero. She does not know he respects her.

9. A moment of danger for either main character results in the realization on the part of the hero or heroine that the feeling between them is true love.

10. A last-minute plot twist threatens their relationship.

11. The two finally communicate and admit their true love, which will last forever.

Why is the reader fascinated by this formula? It tells her that she can have the romance she was brought up to believe in; that her life can be exciting and happy; that she is desirable sexually; that true love lasts forever.

The novels also fulfill her sexual fantasies. Throughout each romance she can imagine taming a devilish man who first lusts for her, then respects and loves her. She doesn't mind knowing the outcome of the plot. In fact, she wants to. It's the satisfying ending she wants to believe in. The formula is unbeatable.

First Step—The Tip Sheet

Each publisher has a different approach to the category, so you as a writer must send a self-addressed stamped envelope (SASE) to the publisher of your choice, asking for a tip sheet that will give you that publisher's requirements. Your letter will be addressed to the editor of that particular series, for example: Editor, Candlelight Ecstasy Books, Dell Publishing Company, etc. You can get the publishers' addresses either from the reference book *Literary Market Place (LMP)* in your library or from the current *Writer's Market* in your local bookstore. (See Appendix A for a list of current romance publishers.)

A good tip sheet will tell you the requirements for a certain publisher. Some sheets are much more detailed than others. If, for instance, you want to write a Gothic romance, you will be told to omit the occult, or to use the occult, or to have any ghostly happenings explained away logically. The ages of the hero and heroine will be specified. You will be told what type of heroine is desired and whether first- or third-person point of view is preferred. If a second man or woman is to figure in the story, you will be informed of this and the role that character will play. The location, in general, will be suggested, as will the amount of sex that is permissible. Finally, you will learn the precise number of words your story is to be. Since each editor's needs vary, the tip sheet is essential to the writer.

Most publishing companies put out a tip sheet for each romance line they handle. Some editors of contemporary lines say that tip sheets are a thing of the past. They prefer to *tell* authors what they want or to send "guidelines." Don't be dismayed. No matter what form the requirements take, formula romances are just that. Discarding tip sheets and pretending no formula exists or calling the novels "mini-mainstream" does not make blockbusters out of series romances.

Types of Category Romances

In a competitive field such as romance fiction, editors closely watch what the readers want, what the competition is doing, and whether or not an innovation is successful. Romance formulas are therefore not static. Since you as a writer must adhere to current trends, the burden is placed upon you to send for the latest tip sheets, to subscribe to romance periodicals, and, whenever possible, to hear editors, writers, and agents speak. (See Appendix B for a list of periodicals.)

The following are basic requirements for various types of romances. Certain information, such as length, will probably remain the same, but changes can occur at any time. Each category is handled in detail in individual chapters.

1. The Traditional Romance. These are the pure, sweet, modern romances with a young, isolated heroine (eighteen to twenty-three) and an older hero (thirty to thirty-five). The love scenes are concerned with kissing and caressing, with marriage a necessary result. The stories are set in contemporary times, are rife with misunderstandings, and stress local food, dress, and customs. They run from 55,000 to 65,000 words.

2. *The Regency Romance.* These tales take place in the British Isles, usually England, between 1811 and 1820, when the Prince of Wales (later George IV) acted as regent for his mad father, George III. The social scene is elegant, with a stress on manners and fashion. The heroine is young (seventeen to twenty-three) but independent, and the hero is older (in his thirties). Flirting takes place, but no explicit sex occurs. The plots are lighthearted, and the dialogue is witty. The length is usually between 55,000 and 60,000 words.

3. *The Gothic Romance and Romantic Suspense.* These stories may be placed in any period as long as the mood is eerie and the setting isolated. Occult happenings may occur if a logical explanation is presented at the conclusion. Romantic suspense stories contain more mystery and less of the ghostly. Both types include little violence and what does occur, takes place offstage. The heroine is young (eighteen to twenty-five), and is usually pursued by two attractive men, the villain and the hero. The latter is older (in his thirties), complex, and moody. The couple is usually too busy solving mysteries to be involved in passionate sex scenes. These books can be any length, depending on the line.

4. *The Gay Romance.* These novels are individual in treatment. The few written so far follow mainly the Gothic trend, with a young lover (eighteen to twenty-five) pursued by an older lover of the same sex (thirty to forty). The love scenes are sensuous rather than explicit. The novels can be longer than series romances, the length suiting the story itself.

5. *Series Historicals.* Similar to Regencies in length (55,000–60,000 words) and type of characters (young heroine, older hero), this tale may be set in the Napoleonic period (1804–1815), the Victorian period (1837–1901), or

the Edwardian period (1901–1910), and will sometimes be termed Regency. These stories, however, tend to be "Harlequins in hoopskirts" rather than comedies of manners.

6. *The Historical Romance.* The term has come to be interchangeable with "bodice-ripper," those romances with a good deal of sex, including rape scenes; but it can refer to any romance that takes place in the past. The category formula is indebted to Margaret Mitchell's *Gone With the Wind* (Macmillan) for its fiery heroine and complex hero. A second man will usually play the villain, though it is possible to confuse hero and villain at first. The story will be tied to an important historic event, such as a war, and will usually be long, from 100,000 to 200,000 words.

7. *Romantic Soaps.* Soaps are introspective, dramatic stories dealing with family tragedies. A "tent-pole" character, often an older member of the family, holds the various elements of the story together. The author goes into each character's mind and uses many flashbacks in these slow-moving stories that run about 75,000 words.

8. *Romantic Sagas.* Usually generation stories, sagas are about exciting events and often depict a family's rise and fall. Ideally the family is rich and powerful, and northern European. The stories often start in the nineteenth or early twentieth century so that one generation can build upon another. They run from 100,000 to 200,000 words and are told in several parts.

9. *The Contemporary Romance.* These stories come in a variety of lengths (55,000–90,000 words) and types. They differ from the traditional romance in several respects. They include more sex and the union can be consummated before marriage. Depending upon the line, the heroine can have sex with someone other than the hero. The heroine can have an impressive job, such as president of her firm. She is no longer isolated. The fear of the hero's ravishing her is not present, since both are now mature adults and close to the same age. The two can now be widowed or divorced. Some lines have heroines who are older (in their forties). Another trend is to have the stories set in the

United States. Several lines are including ethnic heroes and heroines. The main tension, as in all the categories, is sexual; it is achieved through misunderstandings, not social problems. The aura of romance is still paramount.

10. *Young Adult Romance.* These romances are geared for readers from age twelve to fourteen with heroines of fifteen or sixteen and heroes of seventeen or eighteen. The heroines are from typical middle-class backgrounds and lead wholesome lives. The emphasis is on the first romantic relationship, and usually the first kiss is uppermost in the girl's mind. The settings are those normal for a U.S. teenager, and minor characters are included in the form of friends, teachers, parents. These are not the lonely girls of the traditional romances. The stories run from 35,000 to 55,000 words.

Second Step—The Analysis of Novels

You have probably been reading the type of novel that most interests you. If not, start reading. See what other authors are doing. Pay particular attention to unusual situations the authors create and to the characters' reactions within those confines. Formula writing can be difficult in that the pattern is basic and each writer must find an unusual approach to the usual. To keep a reader who already knows the ending interested is not an easy trick; yet that is exactly what the romance writer must do.

If you were drawing from the human figure, you would not omit a study of bone structure. Similarly, don't neglect the *outline* in studying or in writing. Pick a few of your favorite romances and outline them. Go back to the author's starting point and examine the skeleton. What bones are there?

1. Is the beginning striking?

2. Do the hero and heroine meet early in the story, and do they react to each other chemically?

3. Are their reactions properly motivated?

4. Do they have logical misunderstandings?

5. Are the clever things they say to each other put in dialogue form, or are we merely told that clever things have been said?

6. Do any supporting characters promote the plot? What are their roles? Do they overshadow the hero and heroine?

7. Is the heroine's mind continually confused about her feelings for the hero?

8. Is there enough sexual suspense? Are all events based upon the sexual reactions? Does the sex move the plot?

9. How is variety of plot achieved? What unusual twists are there?

10. How is the reader kept aware of the exotic setting?

11. Does the reader continually sympathize with the heroine and hero, even in a rape scene?

12. Is the conclusion logical, and is it happy?

Third Step—Planning the Romantic Ambiance

The pervading romantic atmosphere is of special appeal to the romance reader, so the romance writer takes a special approach. Whereas an author of other types of novels might usually start with theme, plot line, or characters, setting makes a good starting point for the romance. Where the characters are dictates what you will do with them. Characters in a lazy Mediterranean town are not going to act like those in a cold, wet English industrial city. Is it a setting in which the characters will be at work, or are they on holiday? These details will dictate how the major characters interact, what minor characters may be brought in, and how they will be put to use. Often, too, an editor is looking for a particular setting for variety.

American romance writers have until recently been hampered by the insistence on foreign settings. Now, settings in the United States are desirable, and you may write about what you know best. Scenes ring true when the author knows them well and knows the types of people populating the area.

The setting at first need not be glamorous. The heroine sometimes has little money, and the story may be set where she lives or works. In Anne McCaffrey's *Ring of Fear* (Dell), Nialla shows horses and lives mainly on peanut butter. The hero, always wealthy, makes the setting more glamorous. In McCaffrey's story, the two marry and go to his home, which is obviously expensive, with land, stables, pool, and guard dogs. Even if the story takes place in a comfortable English village, the hero may have a manor house nearby. Wherever you place your story, remember that just as the hero's love is reflected in the heroine's beauty, so his presence adds elegance to any setting.

Gothics need not be set in the past, though many are. In these tales the author is striving to convey a mood of mystery. Mood takes precedence over glamour, and the setting may be dingy if the feeling of doom pervades the tale.

Romances are sometimes described as a combination cookbook, travelogue, and fashion magazine. This is not a bad idea for you as writer to keep in mind. Your reader wants to vividly live the scene. Readers are escaping into your story, so they want to see each elegant detail of the lavish background. They want to imagine wearing the brocades and satins and laces they don't wear themselves. They also want to eat the sumptuous meals that the heroine is enjoying. They don't want to be left out of a single detail as they live this romantic experience. For these novels, the trappings are almost as important as the plot. You are creating the romantic ambiance. The story has been told many times.

Now that you have read and outlined stories and have sent for tip sheets, you are more aware of the time period that interests you. Later chapters give specific requirements for the various categories: Regency, Gothic, historical, contemporary, young adult, and gay. You will need a different approach for each type of romance.

III

The Romantic Heroine and Hero

The Heroine's Identity

Who will your heroine be? How old is she? What is her status—orphan, governess, actress, president of a firm? What goal in life is she working toward, or what problem is she trying to sort through? This goal or problem helps to give her an identity and an interest other than the hero. She is a cheerful, spunky person, quite all right without the hero; but he enters, he adds perfection. To appear strong, she must start with a life outside that with the hero, and her goal must not be to find him.

If the heroine has been widowed or divorced, the pain of that experience should usually be out of the way. If the former husband is in the picture, she is over her love for him and feels some other emotion, such as pity. The reader does not want to be reminded of "lost love" but rather of "new love."

An old lover or even the villain, who has earlier raped the heroine, may have affected her psychologically; and sexual tension may result as the hero tries to overcome her resistance. However, the heroine usually is readily able to put a past romance or rape from her mind and approach the future in high spirits.

The Heroine's Vulnerability

The heroine of most romances is vulnerable. She is often much smaller than the hero, tiny against his massive frame. If she is tall, like some of Georgette Heyer's Regency heroines, he is usually taller. The suggestion is always present that he could, if he so desired, rape her; that she is in his power.

A hero is rarely short, but Anne McCaffrey in *Ring of Fear* has been able to portray a short hero who is masculine and masterful:

> I was close enough now to see the light dusting of black hair on his tanned arms and across the muscular plane of his chest, making a thin line down the ridge of the diaphragm muscles, disappearing into the excuse for a bikini he was wearing, which barely covered nature's compensation for his lack of stature.
>
> There was a satisfied expression in his eyes when I jerked mine back from where propriety decreed a well-bred miss ought not to look. He looked suddenly so knowing, so smug, that he was no longer an *objet d'art,* but man, male, masculine. . . .

He soon shows that he is able to rape her if he wishes.

To add to the drama of the heroine's vulnerability, she usually is alone in the world, with few people to depend upon. Also, few people, if any, would ask questions if she were to disappear. This isolation creates suspense.

In Kay Thorpe's *Lord of La Pampa* (Harlequin Presents), the blond heroine from England has not made connections with her dance troupe in Argentina. She signs on as a cocktail waitress, only to learn that she is expected to entertain the men more intimately. The hero rescues her by buying her time, then asks her to marry him so he can collect his rightful inheritance. She is alone in the world. What can she do? He reminds her that the nightclub owner has taken her on his payroll:

". . . he will expect suitable return. Should it be denied him he may find other ways of extracting a profit. You have heard of the white slave traffic?"

Giving the heroine no choice in the matter keeps the reader sympathetic toward her. The sexual undertones of this scene are obvious, and it is dramatic to think she has just been saved only to be victimized.

If the heroine has a supportive family, its members are usually geographically remote, making it easier for the hero to hire or abduct or marry the heroine. The family may simply be financially unable to help the daughter, as in Richardson's *Pamela,* in which the parents lack power to confront the ·gentleman abductor.

The youthfulness of the heroine can also add to her vulnerability. To the hero's thirty or thirty-five, she can be as young as seventeen, too young to have had a past. This age difference helps to ensure that she is a virgin, and the suggestion is that she is therefore more desirable and, again, more vulnerable.

In some romances, especially contemporaries such as Dell's Candlelight Ecstasy line, the heroine is not a virgin. This fact does not mean that she has experienced the ultimate in love. Her earlier sexual experiences could have been unsatisfactory because of a lack in the husband or lover. Even if her sexual experiences have been satisfactory, no man's lovemaking can compare to that of the hero.

The Heroine's Spunk

Despite her defenselessness, the heroine has an indomitable spirit which eventually makes it possible for her to win the

hero. He attempts to conquer her physically, never suc-
ceeding, since she resists him. She conquers him emotionally, and love rules the field.

The heroine is always spunky. (See Chapter 4, "Character Portrayal.") Events that would leave the rest of us
limp never cause her to be sorry for herself. This nonsen-
timental, direct approach to life is appealing to the reader.
No matter how weak the heroine may appear on the surface, underneath she is persevering and courageous.

The Heroine's Appearance

Your heroine need not be beautiful. In fact, she always becomes more beautiful because of the glow of love. The second Mrs. de Winter in Daphne du Maurier's *Rebecca* (Doubleday) is plain. That she suits the hero and that the
readers believe he cares are what counts. Often the Gothic
governess is a mousy girl who blossoms under the sardonic
smiles of the hero.

The Heroine's Struggle

In a romance, whether a period piece or a modern story,
the struggle is mainly in the heroine's mind. For some reason, either because the hero appears to have been leading
a fast life or because he has values that in some way conflict with those of the heroine, she sees him as a menace to
what she stands for. She is not going to change her standards; nevertheless, she cannot help but be attracted to him.
She desires him and at the same time fears him. Because
she fears him, she resents him. Her conflicting feelings for
him are actually the plot of the story. You can readily see
that few minor characters are involved, nor need they be
developed to any extent.

That the heroine does not understand the hero creates
much of the suspense. How will they ever get together
when they continually misinterpret each other's actions?

Marilyn Granbeck in *Maura* (Jove) is careful to spell out her heroine's confusion:

> Maura took an amazed breath. She had a lot to learn about Duggan Quinn! She realized he could have killed Braxton easily but had not done so: he'd preferred to fight on even terms. Duggan became more of an enigma with each new facet she glimpsed.

The Heroine's Point of View

The story is told through the heroine's eyes and almost always in the third person singular. This means that the author describes scenes using "he" and "she" rather than "I," but can know only what the heroine can know. This point of view, as does first-person point of view, forces the writer to live the story through the heroine and forces the reader to do the same, thereby gaining a feeling of immediacy.

In Amii Lorin's *The Tawny Gold Man* (Dell Candlelight Ecstasy), the heroine can feel herself blush, but she can't see it:

> Anne felt an angry flush of color flare in her face as he studied her with amused insolence, his eyes seeming to strip her of every stitch of clothing she was wearing.

This point of view is also effective for sex scenes, as we see in a later passage of the same novel:

> Slowly, reluctantly, his lips released hers, moved over her face and she felt her breath quicken as he dropped feather-light kisses across her cheeks, on her eyelids, and along the edge of her ear.

At times the author uses a different point of view and it works. In *The Reluctant Duke* (Dell Candlelight Regency), I use the omniscient point of view, going into the minds of various characters, showing their reactions to the heroine. This point of view is not on tip sheets, but to achieve a certain effect—in this instance to emulate a comedy of manners—rules are sometimes broken. (See Chapter 12, "The Regency Romance.")

In *The Unknown Mr. Brown,* by Sara Seale (Harlequin Romance), we look at the heroine through someone else's eyes:

> "Understood what?" she asked vaguely.
>
> "The arrangements that have been made for your future," the lawyer replied impatiently. Really! The child could look almost half-witted at times with that wide, unblinking stare and the mousy hair dragged back from those prominent ears, giving her a skinned appearance.

A change in point of view is more often seen in a longer romance. Suspense can be created by showing how another character, the hero perhaps, sees the situation and by our *not* knowing for a time what the heroine is thinking. Perhaps we learn something the heroine should know and does not. We are tense in our desire to inform her. Sometimes scenes in which the heroine cannot take part, such as a battle, should be shown to the reader for plot movement or authenticity. Nevertheless, we are in the heroine's mind for the sex scenes, experiencing them through her.

Switching from one point of view to another takes place gracefully if you change at a break in the story and remember to stay with the new character for a time. Starting a chapter with a fresh viewpoint and remaining in that character's eyes for the entire chapter is a good approach. For the major part, you will show only what one character, your heroine, can see; then for brief intervals, usually in longer works, you may focus on the scene from another character's eyes. Changing points of view in a short novel will usually lessen the intensity and cohesiveness of the work as a whole.

How can you convey what the heroine looks like when using third-person single point of view? The most facile way is through a mirror. She might look at herself, wondering how she will appear to the hero. She might be sitting at the kitchen table and see herself reflected in the toaster; or she might pass a shop window that throws back her reflection. Another approach is to have her think about her looks. She sees how lovely the "other woman" is and wishes she herself didn't have red hair and fair skin that freckles easily.

Other characters look at your heroine, and their glances say a great deal. Dialogue, too, will establish how she looks. The comments of others will portray her in a more lively fashion than will flat description. She might overhear a remark, or something might be said in her presence, as in the following comment from Iris Bancroft's *Rapture's Rebel* (Pinnacle).

> She pulled the gown over her nakedness and then stood quietly while Alexei buttoned it up the back. He took the necklace from his pocket and fastened it around her throat. Then he stepped back and gazed at her with unconcealed admiration. "You are so slender—so delicate. I had trouble finding a gown among those left in the town that would do honor to your fine figure." . . . She basked in the wonder of his appreciation. "You look magnificent!"

The Character's Vantage Point

As we see things from a character's point of view, we also see them through that character's eyes. If it is the heroine, and she stoops, she will be looking up at what she sees. If she is on the rung of a ladder, she will be looking down. If you have created a tiny heroine, she can't see things from the height of a taller person. Instead, she will tend to look up at people or objects. If she sits in a large chair, will her feet have trouble touching the floor? Will this posture make her feel awkward, especially with the hero in the room?

If you change points of view, you must be sure to change vantage points. For instance, in *Tanya* (Gallen/ Pocket), Muriel Bradley enters the eyes of the wicked Count Podyuney as he views the tall, slender heroine. The count twitches with delight at the contemplation of showing Tanya the gallery:

> While this glorious creature looked at the canvases, he himself could look at her. Just far enough to where those lovely breasts began. For he was shorter than she, and sometimes, as in the present situation, this could be to a man's advantage. He did not care about dancing and was not very good at it, but later . . . he could teach her the waltz, hold her in his arms, and, owing to her height and his lack of it, smother his face in the flowers of her bosom.

The Complex Hero

The setting and the heroine help to dictate who the hero will be, and he comes rapidly onto the scene. Though he is usually about ten years older than the heroine, this does not always need to be the case. In Jocelyn Day's *Glitter Girl* (Jove Second Chance at Love), the hero and heroine were in school together and knew each other well before the heroine married a wealthy man and moved away. Now she is back in town, where her first love has become financially successful. But does he trust her to love him for himself rather than for his wealth? Here their similar age is effective.

In period pieces, an age difference is more natural than in a contemporary story. Also, in the Harlequin Romance type of story, the young innocent needs someone older on whom to depend. In the racier contemporary, an age difference is no longer necessary. The heroine portrayed as older is more likely to have a career and is less likely to need an older man to direct her. Today, the two leads can come together as equals.

That the hero is wealthy is never what basically attracts the heroine. But, let's face it, a rich man is the man he is because he has had the power to make money, so that power drive is part of what attracts her.

The hero is a combination of Mr. Darcy in *Pride and Prejudice* and Rhett Butler in *Gone With the Wind*. He appears proud, disdainful, certainly sure of himself, strong, and virile. His outer demeanor cloaks a man who is complex and, most important, loving. But his gentle nature has been carefully masked, perhaps because life has jaded him, perhaps because he carries a deep hurt from the past. Here is mystery.

The chemical reaction between hero and heroine is at once apparent to the reader. Laura London describes Katie's meeting the hero in *The Bad Baron's Daughter* (Dell Candlelight Regency):

> He was the most attractive man Katie had ever seen. Once, as a little girl, when Katie's father had been teaching her how to ride, typically on far too large and temperamental a horse for her tiny size, he had sent her to jump a five-barred gate. The horse had refused, sending Katie flying to the ground with a force that drove the air from her lungs. She felt that same breathless confusion now, as the crowd parted to allow her a clear line of sight.

The sensuality of the horse imagery adds to the power of the description.

At this stage of a story, the hero and heroine feel worlds apart. He looks down on her as an utter innocent—or a schemer, for such goodness cannot possibly ring true to him. She, on the other hand, sees the hero as one who scorns her for her youth or lack of position, or some other reason of which she is unaware.

His scorn for her is apparent mainly through his smiles, which are *mocking, caustic, ironic, sardonic, superior,* and/or *frustrating*. His sensuous lips are continually curling into one of the above. However, you needn't always define the smile. When Thomas in *The Reluctant Duke* comes to propose to Catherine, he cannot help noticing her younger sister, Julia:

> While this exchange was going on, the Duke raised his quizzing glass to look more closely at this younger

sister who appeared so lively. The mother thought she caught a slight smile on his lips, but what it meant she could not tell.

As the romance progresses, the heroine often depends upon the hero, whether wishing to or not. If she is in danger, she is sometimes saved in spite of herself. She usually sees *him* as the danger and often sees another man as the one who can help her. That she has the situation reversed is obvious to the reader.

How can the reader trust the hero, even though the heroine does not? Obviously, we can recognize him anywhere. The more sadistic he acts, the more certain we are that there is a heart of gold (not to mention a bank account) beneath the surface. As a writer, you can't let reader recognition take the place of your work. You will show the heroine's uncertainty as she reacts to his actions. If he kisses her lovingly, she is certain he is dreaming of the other woman. If he is kind to her, she thinks he is mocking her. A certain willfulness on her part to deceive herself is evident. She sees him as out of her sphere and seems to be thinking, subconsciously, "He's too good to be true. If I believe in him, he'll turn back into the frog." Paradoxically, by rejecting him she keeps the prince at her side. The more she rejects, the more fascinated he becomes.

No matter how she reacts, the hero must save her from some unfortunate situation, such as a fire or other accident, or he might save her from her own misconceptions. Sometimes he saves her from both. Often, she saves *him* at some point in the story.

Unusual Roles

In deciding upon your characters, you need not give them conventional roles. Masquerading is popular. The heroine dresses up as a boy in Violet Winspear's *Satan Took a Bride* (Harlequin Presents) and as a highway robber in Freda Michel's *The Machiavellian Marquess* (Fawcett). Using mistaken identity is a good way to build suspense. The hero treats the disguised heroine in a particular way and is puzzled when she doesn't react as he had expected. If she dresses like a boy, as in the two examples above, the hero has the fun of finding out she is decidedly feminine.

In Margaret Rome's *The Girl at Danes' Dyke* (Harlequin Romance), the heroine is suffering from amnesia. A heroine's having amnesia can create suspense in that she can know only what the hero tells her about the extent of their previous relationship, and, of course, she doesn't trust him. Rome, in a clever plot twist, has the hero mistrust the heroine, whom he doesn't know, and her claim of remembering nothing.

The hero plays a pirate in Samantha Lester's *Love's Captive* (Dell Candlelight Regency), and even a ghost in Elizabeth Mansfield's *The Phantom Lover* (Berkley). By giving your characters roles that are unusual yet believable, you can add fresh plot excitement.

Something in Common

The hero and heroine should have something in common other than a mutual physical attraction. They can be in the same field of work, in related fields, or in a social environment in which they would be apt to meet, or they can have mutual interests of some sort. It is not plausible for Mr. Right to have rugged good looks and nothing but a large bank account to share with the heroine—not in a story about true love. Giving the two nothing to share would also make a dull story. Whether the hero is kidnapping her, as in Violet Winspear's *The Awakening of Alice* (Harlequin Presents), in which the hero mistakes the heroine for her sister and forces her to join him on a Greek island, or whether he acts as her boss, controlling and intimidating her, as in Jayne Castle's *Gentle Pirate* (Dell Candlelight Ecstasy), the reader must believe the two are basically compatible because they have some goals or interests in common. We also learn they are a good match emotionally, since she is courageous and he is daring. We get proof along the way that they're a good match sexually; so the usual trials of a marriage—problems with sex, in-laws, and money—will not be present in the final union, and we can believe it will last.

IV

Character Portrayal

I N depicting your characters, you will use two approaches: revelation and development. The romance that depends only on revelation will not be as strong as the one that shows the development of either the heroine or the hero, or both. You will not thoroughly develop the minor characters.

Character Revelation

Revelation differs from development in that to start with, each character has certain traits. We cannot know a character immediately, nor should he or she be completely revealed at the outset. Through proper techniques, you will gradually let the reader know what your characters are already like:

1. Action and reaction. The various stages of plot reveal the hero and heroine to each other as well as to the reader.

For instance, in the "cute meet" (see Chapter 6, "Developing Your Story"), her cool reaction to his aloofness might reveal to the hero that she is prudish, a cold person, or that she doesn't like him; and it might reveal to the reader that she, at this point, thinks he could never be interested in her.

2. *Dialogue.* What the characters say tells us what they are like. What others say about them also reveals a great deal. (See Chapter 7, "Meaningful Dialogue.")

3. *Manner.* The hero is sure of himself, sophisticated, polished, grave. The heroine is sometimes clumsy but more often graceful, vivacious, and always spunky. Their manners not only reveal what they are like but also cause the essential plot misunderstandings.

4. *Thoughts.* We can usually enter only the heroine's mind, but her thoughts can disclose how she perceives the world. They can also add suspense, as she misinterprets the hero's thoughts.

5. *Values.* The heroine wants true love and will not settle for less. The hero appreciates her for her standards, revealing his own character.

6. *Parallelism and contrast.* The heroine and hero usually contrast in attitude, causing friction. Minor characters reveal character traits of the heroine and hero. The "other woman," by contrasting with the heroine, sets her apart as natural, enjoyable to be with, and a person with values. The "other man," by contrasting with the hero, shows the latter as virile, kind, and gentle. Parallel minor characters can also point to character traits of the main characters. More often, romance writers work with contrast, thereby making the heroine and hero appear almost perfect.

7. *Possessions.* What we own tells a great deal about us. However, the heroine owns very little. Her appreciation of the hero's possessions shows her good taste; but she has a lack of interest in amassing material goods. It is the other woman or man who wants possessions and is possessive.

8. *Clothes.* What the heroine and hero wear shows their sense of style. For period pieces, describe clothes in detail,

but for contemporary romances, describe them in general terms. Styles change rapidly, and even names of articles such as *bikini* can date a novel. Women's boots go in and out of style. Heights of heels and lengths of skirts vary. You can be specific by occasionally using a brand name that tends to remain the same over the years despite changes in styles.

Use colors and materials rather than style details to help the reader visualize contemporary garments. Instead of dressing your heroine in a mini- or calf-length skirt, show her in a silk dress that clings to her body in all in the right places. Mention the color to help the reader visualize. Actually, polyester is more apt to cling, but synthetic fabrics are never used. Dress your heroine in natural materials—wool, cotton, linen, silk, cashmere—indicating that she is a person who is natural and has good taste.

If she has little money for apparel, she nevertheless instinctively knows how to wear clothes. Since the hero has money, he has all the best labels, and he usually knows what will look best on the heroine.

In the evening, put the heroine in something diaphanous. She needs little, if any, jewelry; but give her diamonds, not rhinestones. Better yet, let the hero supply them.

Describing clothes in an entertaining way takes practice. Describing contemporary clothes without dating your material is doubly difficult.

Character Development

As the heroine progresses through the story, her character should be developing. In Meredith Kingston's *Aloha, Yesterday* (Jove Second Chance at Love), Christine gradually changes from a drab young widow to the sensual person she potentially is, knowing much more about who she is and what she wants out of life. Since the story is seen from the heroine's eyes, it is usually she who experiences the growth, and the reader experiences it with her. This growth makes the incidents that occur between the hero and heroine convincing.

Since all heroines must be spunky, and attractive, and have a set of values, you will find it difficult to keep your own heroine from becoming a stereotype. But a *gradual growth in her character* as well as her *striving toward a goal* can help to distinguish her within the romantic genre.

Sometimes a character awakens. In Amanda Preble's *Half Heart* (Dell Candlelight Romance), Valerie learns what true love actually is and then is able to say goodbye to a past "love" and lead a new life with the proper man for her—her husband.

In some of the lesser romances, the heroine simply awakens to the fact that she loves the hero. However, this realization alone is not dramatic enough to make a memorable story.

The hero is more difficult to characterize. He tends not to grow, but rather to gradually reveal the many facets of his personality. He is more stylized than the heroine, since we see everything through the heroine's eyes and for a long while she does not understand him. How he reacts to her needs reveals what kind of man he is, with tenderness hidden just below the surface.

The hero *can* grow, however. In Jude Deveraux's *Highland Velvet* (Pocket), Stephen learns to appreciate Bronwyn's strength as leader of her people. In this instance, he matures to the point at which he can adopt her clan's name as his own.

Avoiding Pitfalls in Character Portrayal

Editorializing will be your first approach in describing your characters. You will want to tell us that the hero is handsome and that the heroine is adorable. You will be firmly convinced that adjectives ladled into your story, like chicken soup to the invalid, will bring the scene to life.

Slowly, painfully, drawing lines through all those "lovely" adjectives, you will learn that superimposing your views on the story will detract. If you describe a character correctly, the reader will be able to form her own judgment as to quality.

At first, you will be equally generous with adverbs in describing your heroine's behavior, certain that opening your sentences with modifiers—*frantically, embarrassedly, questioningly, agonizingly*—will give them power.

Your first attempt at characterization will probably result in a heroine who is too sweet and sentimental. She will be more sugary than Pollyanna. You aren't alone in approaching the heroine this way. That she is good does not mean she is not sarcastic or feisty. She should speak up for herself and hold her own with the hero, who is a man of the world. Your first hero is apt to lack the necessary complexity and may merely stand quietly as he smiles ironically. Spend time getting to know the protagonists before putting them on paper.

When you start to move your characters about, your problem will be with anatomy. Be sure a character could make the movements you describe. If the heroine slumps to the ground, are her movements possible? You may find that a body doesn't bend in the way you describe. Do remember that arms and legs remain attached to the body. Sex scenes, especially, can find the couple in positions described in no manual. Studying plays and concentrating on movements that accompany dialogue and silences, revealing character, will enrich your talent. Knowing how people move will help you to accurately express their personalities and sometimes their deeper, more hidden, character traits.

Since character-portrayal errors are pretty standard for beginning romance writers, before you start a novel, practice character sketches, putting your characters in a variety of situations and attitudes:

1. Dress the heroine and hero.
2. Describe his possessions and her reactions to them.

3. Show the hero acting and the heroine reacting to him.

4. Show her reacting to and contrasting to a minor character.

5. Show her embarrassed by the hero.

6. Show her standing up to the hero.

7. Show her thinking about the hero.

8. Show the heroine defending her own values.

Before you can know your characters fully, you must name them. The following chapter will give you some approaches to choosing the correct romance names.

V

What's in a Name?

Two men appear in a romance. One is named Brett Sterling; the other is Leland Gunther. Which of these two is the old man philanthropist? Which is the hero?

These characters from Meredith Lindley's *Against the Wind* (Silhouette Books) remind us that names do give character clues. In this story, the heroine Molly, acting for Mr. Gunther, is inspecting a boat that's for sale. The virile man who is showing her the boat does not keep the conversation businesslike:

> "Tell me what you know about this boat," she said.
> "She's a real love," he drawled. "Just the kind I like. Like a good woman she's always full of spirit, ready for action, and she responds right away to good rough handling."

Molly explains that she meant, "How is she built?"

"She's beautifully built," he said, leaning back against the superstructure and scrutinizing her again through half-closed eyes. His look moved up and down her body as he spoke. "She's wide of beam, and just a little bit top-heavy, but she gives a man a heck of a ride."

We have just met the owner of Sterling Yacht Brokerage. After his comments, Molly is doubtful about his identity:

Suddenly the young man pulled up his T-shirt, exposing most of his tanned chest in the process. But what he was trying to call to her attention was the silver buckle on the belt around his waist.

"My initials, see? I'm Brett Sterling."

She forced herself to pull her gaze downward from the massive chest, covered with a fine layer of the same blond curly hair as his head. She stared at the initials.

"How appropriate," she snapped.

In this instance, Lindley combines witty dialogue with name and character revelation.

The Pattern in Romance Naming

In romances, names tend to follow a pattern. The heroes' names contain hard consonant sounds. Your hero will be Brad or Brence, Kurt, Matt, Scott, or even Carson or Caleb. A Jonathan or Gregory or Thomas slips in now and then, usually in the more elegant Regencies or in the Victorian Gothics.

Heroines' names are decidedly feminine, with soft vowel sounds and two or three syllables: Marianna, Deborah, Melissa, Elizabeth, Julia, Alicia. Now and then we find a Kate or Katie, but she is in reality a Katherine. Anne must be spelled with an *e*. Period pieces require names appropriate to the time, which you will find in books of that era. Young adult heroines tend to have names of two syllables that end in *y* or *ie*: Amy, Christy, Laurie, Katie, Jennie.

Surnames often inspire confidence or indicate cruelty or some other negative characteristic, since romance characters tend to be good or bad. The television soap opera *Capitol* shows the lives of the Clegg and the McCandless families. Would you vote for Trey Clegg III or Tom McCandless? Producer John Convoy sees the McCandless name as inspiring confidence.

Since so many romances are written by English authors, Americans have had to accustom themselves to British names that at first might sound odd to the ear. Mary Burchell, a longtime Harlequin author, uses such heroes' names as Evander, Giles, Nigel, Geoffrey, Toby, and Oliver. Her heroines might be Gwyneth or Leone.

Similar Names

Try not to give two different characters names that start with the same initial. For instance, in *The Mysteries of Udolpho,* the eighteenth-century writer Ann Radcliffe gave us the evil Montoni and the evil Count Morano. The similarity of beginning sounds is a problem for the reader. Using names with the same concluding sound, as Richard Peck does in his Edwardian romance *Amanda Miranda* (Viking), causes no confusion.

Finding Names

Naming characters is not easy. When you most want the right name, you rarely think of it. If a good name occurs to you, jot it down at the time.

Iris Bancroft likes occasionally to honor a friend by naming a heroine after her. Bancroft is careful to get written permission first; she then knows that she has a name no one will object to. Be sure that you don't inadvertently use the name of someone you've once known. Naming villains after ex-lovers definitely won't do.

To find names, I use an old pamphlet put out by a diaper company. In it are long lists of unusual names for both boys and girls.

For surnames, the telephone book is a great help. For foreign names, try language books. If you need an English name, use Meredith Kingston's trick of checking the names of composers in the Episcopal hymnals. She thinks words that relate to the land or weather sound staunch and dignified: Fielding, Wilder, Stoner.

Names That Indicate Character

Sometimes an author lets a favorite name lead her into character development. For *P. S. I Love You* (Bantam Sweet Dreams), Barbara Conklin chose "Mariah" from the song in *Paint Your Wagon,* and the name helped her to envision the character. Conklin says, "I couldn't start my book *The Summer Jenny Fell In Love* (Bantam Sweet Dreams) until I had the name right. I don't feel I truly know a character until I know her name."

In *The Reluctant Duke,* I named Viscount Devon, the obtuse mother's boy, Norval. The very sound of his name warns readers that the heroine will not find him appealing. I also wanted to create a contrast between the dignified surname of Devon and the Christian name. Poor Norval does not live up to his title or his family name.

Some good romances have been published with some poor name choices. Nevertheless, put real effort into choosing well. Help your work along with the best names possible.

With your setting, your characters, and their names decided upon, you are now ready to develop your story. You will put these characters in conflict and keep them there.

VI

Developing Your Story

AT this stage you are ready to outline your own story. It helps to make a list of characters, writing down all you can possibly know about each. Then determine the length of your novel by using the tip sheet. I find it helpful to decide the approximate length of chapters and to divide with this in mind, though not keeping to a strict division. The length of chapters is up to the author and depends on the length of her story. Frequent breaks with cliff-hanger endings, through misunderstandings, tend to hold the reader.

See the plot not as a steady flow but as a series of constant ups and downs. Where is the heroine going? What interrupts her? How does she react emotionally? How does she carry on? What sensual feelings does she have? What takes her off her course again? Since the hero and heroine are on center stage for much of the story, if not all of it, numerous conflicts, mainly misunderstandings, move the plot along. The story line will actually be a series of incidents setting off the emotional attraction of the two.

The opening and closing are not too difficult to plan. The place where writers can bog down is the long middle. You will find it takes great skill to handle only two thoroughly developed characters for an entire novel. But you can do it if you plan ahead.

The Outline

The outline or synopsis is what the editor will read first, and all he or she may read before making a decision on your story. Make your outline appealing. You can do this by following several rules:

1. Give your outline an umbrella opening. Indicate in your first paragraph what, in general, your story is about. Your following paragraphs will take up the main points.

2. Always write your outline in the present tense. The story is happening right now. This tense creates a feeling of immediacy.

3. Use the active, not the passive voice. "John throws the knife," not, "The knife is thrown by John." The character is acting, not acted upon.

4. Use vivid verbs. "John's emotions explode," not "John is angry." Don't overwork the verb *to be*.

5. Give as much action as possible in as few words as possible. Don't describe in detail. Save that for the body of the story.

6. Use dialogue in your outline to indicate how you handle it.

7. Give a definite feeling of the mood by using descriptive words and appealing to the senses. If violence will be part of the story, let the editor know it. If passion is inherent, make your editor feel it.

8. Be sure to tell how your plot is resolved.

Remember, each word counts. Rewrite your outline any number of times. Historical romance novelist Marilyn

Granbeck suggests using "cover copy." Look at the amount of material an editor can squeeze onto the back cover of a book. Readers usually pick books by that cover copy.

If you have trouble plotting the story, ask yourself the same questions you would ask as a reader. And be sure to add enough suspense so that the reader will think after each chapter or incident, What happens next? A misunderstanding at the end of a chapter will help to create a cliff-hanger.

The most important suspense to keep in mind is that caused by chemistry. At every stage the hero and heroine react chemically to each other. He smiles sardonically, but his pulse is hammering. She is sarcastic, but her heart is throbbing. This chemical attraction is more intense than in reality and can leave the heroine almost incapacitated. That's all right. The hero is more apt to get what he wants, thereby giving her what she secretly desires. Often a sort of cat-and-mouse game is afoot. In the more explicit novels there is definitely some sadomasochism. The hero wants to ravage his beloved; she wants to be ravaged, and often is. Even the purest of Harlequins hint at the girl's being taken against her will—but is it totally against her will?

Preparing for Sex Scenes

In your outline, plan for the sex scenes. At first you may find yourself getting carried away with the action and forgetting to add the titillating moments readers are watching for. In every scene you plan, ask yourself what sexual excitement is in it for the heroine. Very early in the story she must meet the hero and start reacting to him dramatically; and that pulsing and throbbing will go on throughout the story, even when she's angry with him, which she will be from time to time. If she puts on a new dress, she sees in his eyes that he is aroused, and she is consequently flushed and weak-kneed. If she doesn't put on a new dress, his eyes will undress her, and he is aroused and she is aroused. Sparks fly constantly in these scenes, and careful planning will remind you to ignite them.

Misunderstandings occur even in intimate scenes, so plan for those as well. Violet Winspear has a good example of this in *The Awakening of Alice:*

> His name broke from Alice's lips as his kissing aroused her to a sweet shuddering she couldn't control, but Stefan took it for rejection and thrust her away from him.

Successful Beginnings

Once you start to write, remember that the reader can put the book down unread if the opening does not please. Aim for simplicity and a sense of excitement or urgency. The sooner you can get the reader absorbed in your story, the more likely you are to keep her. A strong emotion, such as fear felt by the main character, often helps the reader to get into the story quickly. Rebecca Stratton's *Isle of the Golden Drum* (Harlequin Romance) starts out:

> Carys had never felt so frightened in her life before and she kept her eyes tight shut, not only in anticipation of the inevitable crash, but also in a silent prayer that they would not be drowned in the vast expanse of the Pacific Ocean that was waiting down there below them.

And Violet Winspear's *Lucifer's Angel* (Harlequin Romance) begins:

> Fay sat gazing at the brand new wedding ring upon her finger—an exquisite ring, fashioned from platinum, with a band of small diamonds encircling it. The autumn sunshine danced in the stones, their glittering beauty filling her with panic rather than pleasure.

Fear need not always be present. Effective description can pull a reader into the story very quickly, as in Serena Alexander's *Rapture Regained* (Jove Second Chance at Love):

> As she walked away from her overheated Land-Rover, Cathy Dawson glanced up at the dark clouds gathered in the sky, then sniffed the moisture-laden air. She stopped, standing as still as a statue, and listened to the birds squawking. Normally throaty and melodious, their cries had turned shrill, coming louder and faster in an urgent cascade of storm warnings. Far off a dog barked. Carried on currents of electrified air, his yelping sounded uncannily clear.

You will notice that in the above examples, things are not as they should be. A plane is going to crash. A diamond ring inspires panic. The birds' songs have turned to squawks. Just as news stories tell us the unusual in the day—the usual we probably have lived through—so romances put us, as readers, on the brink of something about to happen. Action is the key word, and the sooner you suggest action and then plunge into it, the sooner you ensnare your reader.

The Cute Meet

Meredith Kingston stresses the "cute meet." The term was popular for the romantic movie comedies of the thirties, and aptly describes the first meeting of the hero and heroine. In *Aloha, Yesterday,* Kingston's shy, spinsterlike heroine is still in mourning for her husband, who has been dead for two years. Dressed in a dowdy fashion, she has come to the hotel room of a writer who is to do the story of her husband's life. The handsome hero, dressed only in a towel, answers the door, causing the heroine to lose her composure. He, in turn, is put off by her prudishness.

In Kingston's *Winter Love Song* (Jove Second Chance at Love), the heroine meets the hero as he speeds down the ski slope, commanding, "Follow me." She is astounded at the man's similarity to her former husband, Grant, and only at the bottom of the slope does she see that he actually is Grant.

The cute meet should shake up both hero and heroine, putting them off guard. It should be a moment for both to remember and should help to characterize them. Done well, it sets the tone for the entire interaction between the two.

The Moment of Danger

Every woman wants to be saved by her hero or to save or nurse him. To satisfy this craving and add excitement to the long middle of the story, it is helpful, about two-thirds of the way through, to add a moment when a character is in danger. The hero might be wounded in a train crash as in Winspear's *Lucifer's Angel,* be saved from a fire as in Kingston's *Aloha, Yesterday,* or survive an earthquake as in Winspear's *The Awakening of Alice.* Whatever device you use, be sure that the danger moves the plot along by helping the hero and/or heroine to see each other in a clearer light. Danger can also be used to show the character of either hero or heroine. How one acts in a dangerous situation is very revealing. Finally, danger can be used to awaken the heroine to herself and her approach to life.

The Last-Minute Plot Surprise

Because of the moment of danger, the hero and heroine come together; however, the story is not over. A last-minute surprise will occur—a play on an earlier misunderstanding. The hero will suddenly think the moment of danger really proves that the heroine is after his family's money, or the heroine may decide the hero's presence on the scene proves he loves the other woman.

Whatever conflict you choose, motivation for this final twist will start early in your story, for this will be a repetition and variation of an earlier misunderstanding. If the couple can overcome this conflict, the two can handle anything. Shortly after this last plot twist, the two lovers communicate and agree to live happily ever after.

What makes the happy conclusion believable after such a plot twist? With your skill, you have drawn a heroine (possibly a hero as well) who has gradually developed or awakened throughout the story. The heroine finally realizes how wrong she has been about the hero; usually she comes to this conclusion before or because of the moment of danger. That moment then shocks the hero into admitting his love. The last-minute surprise puts them at odds again. That they start to fall into the old pattern of misunderstanding each other but pull out of it, shows that one or both have grown, that they are now ready to live happily ever after. They have worked out the final misunderstanding for themselves without the aid of a third party. Character awakening or growth is the key.

A pistol duel over Julia, the heroine, creates a moment of danger in *The Reluctant Duke,* especially when Thomas is hit in the arm. However, we have a last-minute plot twist when the two combatants insist they were not dueling over Julia. Hurt and humiliated, Julia determines to leave London and return to the country, renouncing Thomas and society.

For the first time, Thomas takes the lead in communicating. He admits that Julia has taught him to laugh at life a little. The two are able to express their love, and the reader believes they are right for each other. They have solved their final misunderstanding and will now be able to relate successfully throughout a long, adventurous future together.

Between the moment of danger and the final resolution, we have an external-internal pattern. The moment of danger is an external circumstance that breaks through the social veneer. The last-minute plot surprise, as in the example above, shows the characters reverting to old habits in misunderstanding external affairs. Having grown, they are able to check themselves, view the facts more objectively, and arrive at an understanding. This internal understanding of the self brings about the final resolution.

The Villain's Fate

In the romance, minor characters traditionally have tended to be either good or bad. The vamp who is after the hero wears long red fingernails and appears to have few redeeming qualities. The handsome other man who appears so good to the heroine is, in fact, a heel.

In *Jane Eyre,* by Charlotte Brontë, Mrs. Reed, who had mistreated Jane in the girl's youth, ends up with three unappreciative children who cause her sorrow. Those children, who also mistreated Jane, end up unsuccessfully. Even Mr. Rochester, the hero, must pay by being maimed because he attempted to marry Jane while he was already married. In Georgette Heyer's *Cousin Kate* (Doubleday), it is Kate who will become Lady Broome, replacing her manipulating aunt. We are back to the folk and fairy tale world in which evil sisters dance on hot coals.

Editors of some of the more recent contemporary romances are asking for more realism, therefore more shades of grey. This approach will help to vary the formula. However, veering too far from fantasy may diminish the romantic aura.

True Love

In escape literature, readers are anxious to leave the confusion of choice behind. They want the guidelines of the romance formula. In the earlier novels, the heroine has firm ideals from which she will not vary. She is Cinderella or Beauty—respected, admired, and *good,* and loved *because* she is good. Virtue is, for a brief moment, rewarded. In the current stories that are more sexually explicit, the heroine still has standards. She desires and finally achieves true love. Tenacity is rewarded. The formula has shifted slightly, making the statement that true love is every woman's right, and if she persists in her search, she will succeed.

VII

Meaningful Dialogue

CHARLES: The last few days have been extremely agitating. What do you suppose induced Agnes to leave us and go and get married?

RUTH: The reason was becoming increasingly obvious, dear.

CHARLES: Yes, but in these days nobody thinks anything of that sort of thing—she could have popped into the cottage hospital, had it, and popped out again.

RUTH: Her social life would have been seriously undermined.

—Blithe Spirit

Dialogue is the best way to bring a story to life, yet it is the most difficult way and the area in which many romances bog down. The trite comment will attract no readers. Your characters should say the clever things the reader would like to say, as in the above Noel Coward example.

On the other hand, dialogue that is not suitable to the character or scene is just as bad as dull dialogue. The more lifelike your dialogue can be while serving a real purpose in the story—such as moving plot, revealing character, or enhancing mood—the more likely you are to write a strong novel. Popular romances have very little narrative, so the dialogue carries the story.

The Purposes of Dialogue

1. To reveal past action. In *Highland Velvet,* Jude Deveraux uses conversation to let us know that the bridegroom is tardy and sorry for it, that the bride was promised by King Henry, and that the soldiers hate the Scots but have been smitten by the Scottish heroine:

> "Had I known," he whispered, "had I any idea, I would have come weeks ago when King Henry promised her to me."
> "Then she meets with your approval?"
> He ran his hand across his eyes. "I think I'm dreaming. . . ."
> "I assure you she is real. Why do you think I keep her guarded so heavily? My men are like dogs ready to fight over her at any moment. They stand around and repeat stories of the treacherous Scots to each other, but the truth is, individually each of them has generously offered to take your place in the girl's bed."

2. To move plot. Romance writers tend to move plot through narration, and often miss a chance to combine action with the emotion revealed in speech. The following scene from *Highland Velvet* takes advantage of dialogue in revealing action:

> "Tell Lord Stephen I will not meet with him."
> "Will not, my lady? You are unwell?"
> "I am quite well. Give my message as I said, then

go to Roger Chatworth and tell him I will meet him in the garden in ten minutes."

The girl's eyes widened, then she left the room.

"Ye'd do well to make peace with yer husband," Morag said. "Ye'll gain nothing by making him angry."

"My husband! My husband! That's all I hear. He is not my husband yet. Am I to jump at his call after he has ignored me these past days?"

3. To suggest future events. The opening of Dorothy Dunnett's *The Game of Kings* (Fawcett) is punctuated with dialogue that crescendoes as each comment adds information. That everyone is making some remark about Lymond's return tells us something about him, as does the description of the way the men's remarks are made, "with contempt and disgust," while we hear "a woman's voice with a different note"; and we anticipate trouble in the future:

"Lymond is back."

It was known soon after the *Sea-Catte* reached Scotland from Campvere with an illicit cargo and a man she should not have carried.

"Lymond is in Scotland."

It was said by busy men preparing for war against England, with contempt, with disgust; with a side-slipping look at one of their number. "I hear the Lord Cutter's young brother is back." Only sometimes a woman's voice would say it with a different note, and then laugh a little.

We find it hard not to attempt to discover what the future holds.

4. To reveal character. In *Forever Amber* (Macmillan) by Kathleen Winsor, Amber's guardians discuss her. Sarah says:

"After all, Matt, she is a lady."

"Lady! She's a strumpet! For four years now she's caused me nothing but trouble, and by the Lord

Harry I'm fed up to the teeth! Her mother may have been a lady but she's—"

"Matt! Don't speak so of Judith's child. Oh, I know, Matt. It troubles me too. I try to warn her—but I don't know what heed she pays me. Agnes told me tonight—Oh, well, I don't think it means anything. She's pretty and the girls are jealous and I suppose they make up tales."

Besides learning that Amber has noble blood, we learn that others don't think well of her behavior. This character revelation forewarns of events to come.

5. *To enhance mood.* Prisoners are escaping in Roberta Gellis's *Winter Song* (Playboy):

"They have closed the door."
"Is it barred?" came a fearful whisper.
"What will we do?" another whimpered.
"How did Ernaldus get out if it is barred from within?" a third cried.

The terror of these men is more believable as they ask hurried questions that no one will answer, than it would be if the scene were merely described. Since the dialogue doesn't completely convey the emotion, the adjectives and verbs must be strong: *fearful whisper, whimpered, cried.* The sound the men make rises in intensity as they realize their plight.

6. *To contribute to setting.* In Carol Norris's *A Feast of Passions* (Pocket), the heroine, along with Jamie, a half-aborigine, is escaping through the rain forest. Showing the effects of this steep terrain on the heroine gives the scene reality:

"Jamie," she whispered toward the sound of his retreating form, "I shall die. I must rest. Truly! I shall fall, and it's so steeeep!". . .

"You not like climbing up. You complain. You

not like climbing down. You find a stone in your mouth, you talk so much."

"But it's damp down here. It's so dark I can't see, and leeches will bite me."

7. To give a sexual undertone.

He smiled ironically. "How little you know your man, *cara*. . . . I do not love you because you fought me but because you are beautiful and intelligent with a great deal of spirit and courage. All these things will remain yours even though you become submissive to my will."

This scene from Rachel Lindsay's *Castle in the Trees* (Harlequin Presents) contrasts words such as *fought, spirit,* and *courage* with *beautiful, intelligent,* and *submissive,* subtly reminding us of the dominant-male theme.

8. To convey passion. The following is the parting scene of Heathcliff and Catherine in Emily Brontë's *Wuthering Heights:*

"What kind of living will it be when you—oh, God! would *you* like to live with your soul in the grave?"

"Let me alone. Let me alone," sobbed Catherine. "If I've done wrong, I'm dying for it. It is enough! You left me too; but I won't upbraid you! I forgive you. Forgive me!"

"It is hard to forgive, and to look at those eyes, and feel those wasted hands," he answered. "Kiss me again; and don't let me see your eyes! I forgive what you have done to me. I love my murderer—but *yours!* How can I?"

The interjected, abrupt phrases—"oh, God!" "Let me alone," "It is enough!"—help to convey the seething passion underneath the words. Notice the funereal terms in the lovers' parting scene: *grave, sobbed, dying, wasted, murderer.* These are set against *living, God, soul, forgive, kiss.*

By taking the mind in disparate directions, the words make us feel that death is wrenching the lovers apart. The mood is truly tense, as each lover tries to convince the other of the depth of his or her love.

9. *To convey humor.* Humor may be used in a romance to relieve the mood of passion, or unrequited love, to make the love seem more joyful, or to reveal character. Often humor is dependent upon surprise: we expect one thing to occur—a character to understand a situation or to act like a thinking human rather than like a robot—and when the character refuses to act as we expected, the jolt causes us to laugh. In the following instance from *The Reluctant Duke,* we expect Norval to understand Julia's machinations. When he does not, the surprise results in humor:

"Of course, I shall dance with Lord Devon," said Julia to Norval.

"It's polite to wait to be asked," grumbled that lord.

"Why, you have been pestering me the entire evening. You know you have." She gave a little laugh.

"Haven't. Wouldn't. You're acting strange again, Julia."

"Come, come, Lord Devon, do not tease so." Julia took his arm and gave it a pinch.

"Ouch. You needn't pinch me."

Julia laughed and fanned herself. "Lord Devon is such a tease, is he not?"

How To Write Potent Dialogue

Conveying Emotion Through Dialogue

Often romance authors describe the way in which a character is talking, rather than letting the dialogue convey the meaning. Let's suppose a character says:

"That's just like you. I'm not surprised."

The line has no specific emotional content. To give it substance, the temptation is merely to add an adverb:

"That's just like you. I'm not surprised," he said caustically.

You can change the meaning of the dialogue with any adverb you choose: *lovingly, angrily, disappointedly.*

Instead, let's change the dialogue to include the emotion:

"That's just like you, Little Miss Prude. I'm not surprised."

Now what is the emotion? Let's make a different change:

"That's just like you, darling. I'm not surprised."

No adverb is needed to convey the feeling of the speaker. Your characters will come to life, as well as your story, if you let them *express* their own feelings, rather than merely *telling* the reader.

Denotation and Connotation

Many words suggest a meaning apart from the literal, dictionary meaning. They *connote* an idea.

1. Rain   *Denotation,* what the word *means*—condensed atmospheric water vapor, falling in drops
Connotation, what the word *suggests*—gloom, sadness
2. Apple   *Denotation*—an edible fruit
Connotation—something desirable: "The apple of his eye," "an apple for the teacher"; something tempting: the symbol of the First Fall

The writer aware of the connotations of words can enrich her dialogue through giving subliminal messages to the reader. Words with the desired connotations add nuances that enhance the romantic aura.

Violet Winspear uses words with implied meanings in
Bride of Lucifer (Harlequin Presents):

> Her soft mouth suffered the aggression of his.
> "Always," he whispered, "you will have virginal
> eyes and a loving mouth. These I want. Deny me ever
> and I shall turn savage."
> "Y-you would never allow me to deny you."
> "You speak of our wedding night?"
> "Yes."
> "Did you hate me as much as you believed you
> would?"
> "No."
> "You awoke wearing the rosary as I promised. The
> pearls lay soft against your skin, and I think I shall
> always remember you like that."

Notice the key word, *virginal*. Is it a strange choice for
a love scene? Think of what it connotes or implies. Then
notice its opposite, another word charged with meaning,
aggression. These two words combined suggest a rape.
Winspear uses further subtle contrasts with *loving, soft, ro-
sary*, opposed to *savage* and *hate*. The pull between opposing ideas and the connotation of those words gives a sa-
domasochistic undertone to the scene. The disparate
implications create tension and, therefore, drama. Could
you underline key words in one of your own passages of
dialogue and find subliminal meaning?

Use of Dialect

Winston Graham in the *Poldark* series sets his love story
against the struggles in a Cornish mining community in
the latter part of the eighteenth century. The dialect of the
townspeople gives the scene authenticity and helps to indicate class:

> Demelza sat up and winced. "Mark Daniel? What
> does he want with me?"

"Nothin' by rights. He come first at noon. They're from home, I says, an'll not be back, she afore supper, I says, an' he afore cockshut tomorrow, I says. Oh, he says, an' goes off an' comes back and says what time did ye say Mistress Poldark would be back, he says, an' I says supper to-night, I says, an' off he d'go wi' his long legs stalking."

We know by Demelza's wincing that she is not glad to hear the news. Her question indicates tension. The rambling, disjointed reply adds suspense, since Demelza (and the reader) wants the answer immediately.

If you choose to use dialect, be sure it's one you know. Don't make up a dialect that is nonexistent.

Natural Speech Rhythms

Characters do interrupt one another or break off in the middle of a sentence or disagree, as in Georgette Heyer's Regency romance *The Nonesuch* (Fawcett Crest):

"Damme if I wouldn't prefer to see you wasting the ready on a pack of ragged brats than on that young once-a-week man!"

"Oh, George, no!" expostulated Sir Waldo. "Coming it *too* strong!"

"Oh, no, I ain't!" said George obstinately. "When I think of the things he said today, and the gratitude he owes you—"

"He owes me none."

"What?" George gasped, once more coming to a sudden halt.

Staccato rhythms—created by the use of one-syllable words, breaks in sentences, and exclamations—increase the intensity of the mood. The specific words have strong consonant sounds that add to the abruptness of the scene: *Damme, pack of ragged brats, gasped,* and *halt.*

Your dialogue will be effective if it not only serves a particular purpose in the story but also is correct for each character. Does it convey class or region or period accurately?

Read your dialogue aloud and omit unnecessary phrases that serve no specific purpose. Weak dialogue is the romance writer's most common error. Don't concentrate on foreplay and afterplay, to the neglect of wordplay!

VIII

Sensuous Description

The Five Senses

IN describing the heroine's feelings, constantly remind yourself to appeal to the five senses. As the heroine tastes the food, the reader tastes the food. As the heroine feels the gorgeous brocades and velvets, so does the reader. Strange sounds attract, or sights astound. The more often you appeal to the senses, the more believable your story will be.

A good practice for such description is to actually use your own senses and write about the experience.

1. Taste. Try a lemon. What is the taste? How does it feel in your mouth? What is your tongue doing as you taste it? What is your mouth doing? Now try a persimmon. What is the taste? Astringent? Sweet? Add another sense. How does it *feel* on your tongue? Slippery? Slithery?

How does your tongue feel after you have swallowed the bite of persimmon?

2. *Touch.* Describe the feel of a smooth piece of wood, of a rough eraser, of a strand of your hair. But do not take the easy adjectives. Have you written anything out of the ordinary?

3. *Sight.* In her poem "Aubade," Edith Sitwell says that the "morning light creaks." Light cannot creak. And yet we know what creaking light looks like. The sensation produced in one modality or point (in this case sound) when another has been stimulated (sight) is called *synesthesia.* Such a surprise can heighten your effect.

4. *Hearing.* Close your eyes and listen to the sounds around you. Alliteration can be an effective way to describe them. This technique is the repetition of a consonant sound such as, "*S*he li*s*tened to the *s*oft *s*lapping of the waves on the *s*hore."

Henry Thoreau in *A Week on the Concord and Merrimack Rivers* (T. Y. Crowell) describes sounds of dogs barking at night, "from the loudest and hoarsest bark to the faintest aerial palpitation under the eaves of heaven." He describes the bark of the terrier, "at first loud and rapid, then faint and slow, to be imitated only in a whisper; wow-wow-wow-wow—wo—wo—w—w." Here he has used *onomatopoeia,* suiting the sound to the meaning.

Can your reader hear the rustle of your heroine's gown or the tapping of her heels on the pavement? Do you prove that your characters exist through the sounds they make or the sounds they hear around them?

5. *Smell.* Don't reserve the use of this sense for food. A man's shaving lotion smells—tell how it smells. Hair has an odor. Skin has an odor. The smell of the hero to the heroine can be powerful in a love scene. Make the scene more potent. Tell us about the *taste* of his mouth on hers. Appeal to more than one sense at a time.

Sense impressions are vital in conveying subtle love scenes. The explicit in sex can be avoided if the senses are aroused—several at once. You want your scene to be both passionate and lifelike.

Metaphor and Simile

A *metaphor* is an implied comparison, thereby aiding the reader in understanding meaning. In *The Awakening of Alice,* Violet Winspear says of Alice, whom the hero has thrust aside, "She felt stunned, like the big white moths who [sic] stunned their wings against the wall lamps. . . ." The abstract feeling of rejection is thereby put into concrete action—the stunned moths—which we can readily visualize.

Keep to a single image when creating a metaphor and extend it, as D. H. Lawrence does with lava imagery in *The Plumed Serpent* (Knopf).

> And he, in his dark, hot silence, would bring her back to the new, soft, heavy, hot flow, when she was like a fountain gushing noiseless and with urgent softness from the volcanic deeps. Then she was open to him soft and hot, yet gushing with a noiseless soft power. And there was no such thing as conscious "satisfaction." What happened was dark and untellable.

One image, lava, extended through the hypnotic repetition of adjectives—*hot, gushing, soft, noiseless, dark;* and a variation of that repetition—"hot silence," "hot flow," "soft and hot"—subtly conveys what is "dark and untellable."

A *simile* is a form of metaphor that makes a comparison by using *like* or *as.* Aldous Huxley, who explores love and sex in *Crome Yellow* (Harper), writes:

> Mr. Scogan was like one of those extinct bird-lizards of the tertiary. His nose was beaked, his dark eye had the shining quickness of a robin's. But there was nothing soft or gracious or feathery about him. The skin of his wrinkled brown face had a dry and scaly look; his hands were the hands of a crocodile. His movements were marked by the lizard's disconcertingly abrupt clock-work speed; his speech was thin, fluty, and dry.

Personification

Personification, giving inanimate objects human attri-
butes, is a favorite device of poets but works well in all
fiction. This device adds variety and intensity to your approach. A clock *telling* the hour has been personified. Objects in an old manor house, *speaking* of doom, are personified. Personification is also used to bring the intangible
into lifelike form, as in Carl Sandburg's poem "Fog," in
which the fog is pictured as a cat.

A character might embody a particular quality, and thus
be the personification of hate or happiness, cowardice or
strength. In a typical romance, the heroine personifies
good; the hero, courage; and the other man or woman,
villainy.

A mistake romance writers sometimes make is to attempt to be both explicit and nonexplicit at the same
time. For instance, rather than naming the hero's male or-
gan, a writer refers to "the hardness of his male desire."
This euphemistic phrase personifies the idea of desire as a
bodily function. (The wording here is less than romantic
and could provoke laughter when no humor is intended.)

Naming Concrete Objects

Concrete objects are specific words such as *rock* or *tree*.
They stand for objects that can be seen or felt. Giving concrete objects specific names so that the reader can visualize
correctly and believe in your scene is effective. Naming
also helps to give a feeling of immediacy. If you want to
say that flowers are in bloom, name one or two: holly-
hocks, daisies, agapanthas. If you want to say that trees
line the drive, name them: elms, eucalyptus, oak. Don't
just write about birds in the garden. Are they robins or
sparrows, blackbirds or mockingbirds?

Symbol

Henry James titled one of his novels *The Golden Bowl,* after his symbol of apparent perfection with an almost imperceptible flaw. Maggie Verver has married Prince Amerigo. Her father has married her good friend, Charlotte Stance. Charlotte and Amerigo resume an affair once dropped because neither had money.

Before Maggie's marriage, Charlotte spends a day with Amerigo and wants to give him a wedding present of a golden bowl. He refuses because it has a crack beneath the surface, and he is superstitious. Maggie later confronts him with the bowl and the earlier rendezvous. She now knows that Charlotte and the prince were intimate:

> . . . the horror of finding evil seated, all at its ease, where she had only dreamed of good; the horror of the thing hideously *behind,* behind so much trusted, so much pretended, nobleness, cleverness, tenderness.

Just as a split under the gold veneer diminishes the value of the crystal bowl, so the secret relationship has endangered Maggie's marriage and that of her father.

Jocelyn Day cleverly uses symbolism in *Glitter Girl.* Before the story opens, the heroine has changed from someone who desires wealth to someone who has more meaningful values. However, after her divorce, she clings to an expensive Jaguar as a form of security. The car, then, becomes a symbol of her continued need for what glitters. When she is able to part with the car, she is ready for a lasting relationship with the hero.

Tone

Sensuous description can be summed up in the word *tone.* It stands for mood and style, or the way in which you express yourself to create a particular aura—in this case, a sensuous, romantic one. You will create your tone by appealing to the senses and using the correct adjectives and adverbs to do so. You will, of course, limit your use of modifiers to those that are essential to create your mood. You will use devices such as metaphor, simile, and personification to heighten the drama of your piece. You will vary the pacing so that some sentences are quick and alert, others slow and languorous. In other words, you will weave a feeling into the structure of your work, as if it were the woof to the warp, thereby creating a distinctive, memorable tone.

IX

The Erotic Sex Scene

ROMANCE is a lyrical, fantasy world of ardor and adventure. The loved one is pure. The lover is devout. But underlying the medieval knight and fair lady trappings is sex. Whether the writer is subtle or more explicit, the popular romance is always a sexual fantasy.

The earlier category romance coupled a hero and heroine, satisfied with a kiss—at least for the first two hundred pages—and there the book ended. Modern morals have changed, and the romance genre has evolved with them. However, in all romances, from the innocent Harlequin Romances to the "bodice-rippers," there are sexual overtones. The heroine desires the hero, and he wishes to ravish her.

We've seen that the moment the heroine meets the hero, she starts chemically reacting to him. Since we are usually in her mind only, we can feel her reactions but not be sure of his. Sometimes her immediate reaction to the hero is unfavorable, as is Rosemary Gallagher's to Lario, an Indian foreman, in Parris Afton Bonds's *Dust Devil* (Fawcett). As the two travel by stagecoach to the ranch in New Mexico, we are told:

> What seemed almost unbearable to her was the unending proximity with the third passenger, the Indian, Lario . . . the contact of their shoulders when the stage hit a rock or his hand at her elbow when she descended from the high step of the Concord coach.

However, by the time their destination is reached, she wonders,

> . . . what was it in Lario's velvety black eyes that burned in her brain so?

Romance writers tend to use the same terminology to show the heroine's reaction to the hero. The heroine "shudders," or "feels dizzy," and the hero displays his "arrogance." Such description can become trite. Nevertheless, notice the heightened effect D. H. Lawrence achieves in *The Plumed Serpent* with the same terms:

> Kate saw the sigh lift the soft, quiescent cream-brown shoulders. The soft cream-brown skin of his back, of a smooth *pure* sensuality, made her shudder. The broad, square rather high shoulders, with neck and head rising steep, proudly. The full-fleshed, deep chested, rich body of the man made her feel dizzy. In spite of herself, she could not help imagining a knife stuck between those pure, male shoulders. If only to break the arrogance of their remoteness.

The use of specific visual words is the main clue to the effectiveness of this passage. We *see* the cream-brown shoulders. Repetition makes them more real and visual. They are "broad," "square," "high." Lawrence's master stroke is the ability to make us see the arrogance, something intangible. The average writer would picture the hero's looking down at Kate, ironically. Instead, Lawrence makes the remoteness palpable through the set of the shoulders and the suggestion that a knife could actually be driven, not just between the shoulders, but into the attitude itself.

Good Taste

Editors ask that sex scenes be in good taste. But what does that mean? Good taste is subjective and its definition will vary from editor to editor, but it usually means that specific parts of the anatomy are not referred to, that some subtlety is employed. For example, in Harlequin Romances, sweeter than the Harlequin Presents line, the words *breast* and *virgin* are taboo. In the more recent contemporary and historical romances the writer has more leeway in use of language, both in sex scenes and in the use of an occasional swearword or vulgarity. Check the types of romances you intend to write to learn what vocabulary is acceptable.

To achieve good taste in love scenes, the writer should appeal to the senses and suggest rather than specify. Suggested action can be more arousing than action spelled out in detail.

D. H. Lawrence is a master at understatement and the use of metaphor. The following is a scene between the Indian hero, Cipriano, and the Irish heroine, Kate, from *The Plumed Serpent:*

> He closed the shutters till only a darkness remained.
> Then in the darkness, suddenly, softly he touched her, stroking her hip.
> "I said you were my wife," he said, in his small, soft Indian voice. "It is true, isn't it?"
> She trembled, and her limbs seemed to fuse like metal melting down. She fused into a molten unconsciousness, her will, her very self gone, leaving her lying in molten life, like a lake of still fire, unconscious of everything save the eternality of the fire in

which she was gone. Gone in the fadeless fire, which has no death. Only the fire can leave *us*, and we can die.

First, Lawrence eliminates the sense of sight through closing the shutters. He then, in darkness, employs the sense of touch, "stroking her hip," and of sound, "his small, soft Indian voice." Next, her emotional and physical reactions to those senses are made tangible through the image of molten metal. In this case, passion is the flame that melts the metal of her will. Lawrence, expanding the image, compares her loss of self to a "lake of still fire." The suggestions of the "eternality of the fire" and the "fadeless fire, which has no death" suggest a hellish intensity, giving another, deeper level of meaning to the image.

Rape and Near-Rape

The most innocent of romances implies that the hero, if he so desires, can rape the heroine. The reader must be aware that the hero is free to do with the heroine as he likes. His size in comparison to hers helps to remind us that he is in control. That he doesn't take advantage of her characterizes him and shows how truly he loves her.

Often the two are entirely alone, as in Barbara Cartland's *Touch a Star* (Jove). During an elaborate Venetian party, the hero takes the heroine to a deserted island on his estate. No help would be forthcoming were she to need it. So the setting in itself creates some suspense while adding to the reader's sexual fantasy.

In Kathleeen E. Woodiwiss's *Ashes in the Wind* the heroine, Alaina, fears the hero. "They were in the house alone, and there was no one to stop him if he chose to take her again." Notice that their situation is spelled out for us.

In most romances there is a touch of sadomasochism. The plot in which the husband or lover rapes his wife or loved one and she enjoys it is not uncommon. Woodiwiss gives us such a scene in *Ashes in the Wind,* in which the hero, Cole Latimer, intoxicated, ravishes Alaina, who makes an unsuccessful attempt to stop him. That she desires him, too, is evident. Moreover, since Cole is drunk, he is not in complete control of his actions. This intoxication is a way of including him in a rape scene and minimizing his responsibility so that the heroine—and readers—can remain sympathetic to him. Moreover, we do not blame the heroine for losing her virtue.

Another familiar plot is one in which the hero holds the heroine captive with the constant threat of rape, a threat that she, while claiming to abhor, actually finds exciting, even fascinating. Violet Winspear in *Palace of the Pomegranate* (Harlequin Presents) goes so far as to have her heroine whisked across the Persian sands by the mysterious Kharim Khan. In one scene, after undressing the heroine so she will not get a desert chill, and roughly drying her with a towel, he says:

> "You deserve the taste of the whip, my little filly, rather than petting—but come, why be shy with me any more? I know how beautiful you are, and you know that I don't intend to let you go. Be kissed instead of bruised. It is far more pleasant, for you, for me."

As he caresses her, she fights back "with all the desperation of a little animal." This fiery spirit fascinates the hero; and out of such tauntings and strugglings comes an ending of true and lasting love. It is just such animal imagery and the idea that the hero loves the heroine because she is beautiful that cause some to condemn the romance as degrading to women and others to read romances.

Near-rapes by the wrong man are also described in a sensuous manner, but he is described in far different terms than is the hero. The villain's breath is disgusting and his kisses wet in Granbeck's *Maura:*

> His weight was overpowering. She was thrown back to the bed and he fell on her, pinning her arms. His

mouth searched wetly. When his lips brushed her cheek, she twisted away. His sour breath sickened her and the intimacy of his body on hers was obscene.

When it is the hero who is drunk and rapes the heroine, Woodiwiss writes about "the brandy taste of his mouth." The touch of the hero's body is desirable even though feared.

The reader must not feel disgusted by the actual rape scene. Early in the "bodice-ripper" romance plot, the heroine is usually raped by the hero; and we must remain sympathetic with both characters. In such scenes, the writer must be especially careful to motivate the actions of the two. These rapes are more acts of passion than of violence, and we mustn't feel as we would while reading about an actual rape.

Though the reader feels good about the scene, the heroine feels guilt and anger. Her emotions make her at odds with the hero, who has caused her to lose control. She will show him she doesn't need him (since she has just shown him that she does). Her pride has been hurt. She also has been reminded of feelings she has not been aware of or has been repressing. Now her confusion of feelings is uppermost in her mind, and she resents the one who has caused such doubt.

Arousing the Reader

Romance writers use strong adjectives and verbs to draw the reader into the love scene. As you write, try adjectives such as *burning, hungering, throbbing, exploding,* or *scalding.* Forget the verb *to be.* Instead, try verbs that convey action or emotion such as *plunged, stroked, caressed, quivered, writhed, pressed, searched, arched,* and *moaned,* to name a few.

When passion subsides and contentment follows, the pace slows and less dynamic verbs take the place of explosive ones. Pacing is important in sex scenes. You as writer may move from short, abrupt sentences to lyrical metaphors to slower-paced moments in which the couple can languorously enjoy each other.

Breathless interjections can lend immediacy as in Charlotte Lamb's *Duel of Desire* (Harlequin Presents):

> He paused, his breathing rapid and harsh. "Did I hurt you? Darling, did I hurt you?"
>
> "No, oh, no," she whispered. Her hands pressed him down to her. "Oh, Alex, darling, I want you so much . . ."
>
> He groaned, his body trembling violently. "Deb. . . . Oh, God, Deb, I love you like hell . . ."

You will learn to allot little time to sex scenes with a woman other than the heroine, and your adjectives in such scenes will not be flattering. She will sound sensuous but not as desirable as the heroine because of your adjectives and verbs. In Granbeck's *Maura,* Beau makes love to Irene:

> Then they were together, hands exploring, mouths tasting, until their bodies met in passion. She clawed at his flesh and writhed, to meet his body. His hard muscles moved under her hands and his mouth stopped her cries until all thoughts were blanketed by exploding pleasure.

Similarly, when the wrong man makes love to the heroine, you will remember to give him less space and see that his sexual prowess does not compare to that of the hero.

Types of Sex Scenes

1. One Desires; One Rejects.

She dreamed and burrowed deeper into a pleasant fantasy of arms slipping about her, a lean male body drawing close. Hands caressed her flesh, pushed down the thin chemise and teased her breasts. She sighed in the dream and opened her thighs to a tender touch.

Consciousness came abruptly and frighteningly. It was not a dream! Someone was beside her in the bed, touching her intimately and expectantly. She pushed savagely at the head nestled at her bosom. She pummeled her fists at the man and opened her mouth to scream. The head jerked up abruptly and there was a startled exclamation. [Granbeck's *Maura*]

2. *Both Desire; One Turns Away.*

He took a deep, shuddering breath, exhaling it slowly, as his palm continued to trace the circle of her hardened nipple. "I want you, Dannee." His voice was quiet and restrained. The look in his eyes told her that he would not make another move until she gave her consent, and frustration welled up in her.

In making her choose, he left her no choice. She couldn't let herself give him what he so obviously wanted—and what she so obviously wanted to give. She covered his hand, removing it from her breast. His other hand brushed aside the tendrils of hair that clung to her forehead as she tried to gather what was left of her pride.

"No." [Rita Clay's *Wanderer's Dream* (Silhouette Books)]

3. *Both Desire; One Misunderstands the Other.*

Tiffany's heart pounded in panic, yet suddenly the cruel grip on her shoulders faded from her consciousness. Instead, she felt the length of his hard, lean body pinning her to the log. The powerful muscles of his thighs straining against the harsh pressure of his pelvis. He shifted his leg, deliberately forcing her knees apart. Something flickered within her, an awakening of something raw and elemental, a primitive force that flamed through her body. She felt an almost instantaneous response in Clay, an electrical awareness, as if a high-voltage spark had arced between them. His hands hadn't moved and yet she felt a swelling response in her breasts, an aching yearning for all the times he had touched them in the past. Her body no longer felt the chill wind; a heat shimmered around them. The cold glint in his eyes had changed to a smoldering glow and the contemptuous twist of his lips was a sensual curl . . .

With an oath he suddenly flung her aside. The abrupt movement threw her off balance and she stumbled to her knees in the sand.

"It won't work any more," he said grimly. "You're not going to twist me around your little finger again." [Day's *Glitter Girl*]

4. The Hero Lusts for the Heroine.

An almost lecherous smile tempted Cole's lips as his eyes swept the bed. He would not have her see it and replaced it with his best ominous frown. He limped forward, moving close behind her, as his hand dipped low to lift the scissors from the sewing kit. His quick fingers pulled out the waistband of her pantaloons, and after a deft snip, they sagged loosely downward. With a startled gasp, Alaina snatched for them and retrieved her modesty, but, with a surgeon's sure hand, Cole reached out to her shoulders and cut through the straps. Unhampered, the shift plunged and was barely caught at the brink. She whirled, an expression of indignation frozen on her face. [Woodiwiss's *Ashes in the Wind*]

5. The Heroine Rejects Sex with the Other Man.

His [Beau's] eyes were defiant and ablaze with lust. He took her swiftly, with a fury that bordered on savagery. And when he was finished, he rolled away and lay with chest heaving and eyes closed.

Maura slid from the bed and, numb with revulsion, kicked aside the torn gown. The sight of Beau's half-naked body made her shudder. [Granbeck's *Maura*]

6. *Both Desire, Yet Come Together, Clashing.*

"I wish I could hold you," she continued bitterly, "till we were both dead! I shouldn't care what you suffered. I care nothing for your sufferings. Why shouldn't *you* suffer? I do! Will you forget me—will you be happy when I am in the earth? . . ."

"Are you possessed with a devil," he pursued, savagely, "to talk in that manner to me, when you are dying? . . . You know you lie to say I have killed you; and, Catherine, you know that I could as soon forget you, as my existence! Is it not sufficient for your infernal selfishness, that while you are at peace I shall writhe in the torments of hell?"

"I shall not be at peace," moaned Catherine, recalled to a sense of physical weakness by the violent, unequal throbbing of her heart, which beat visibly and audibly under this excess of agitation. [Emily Brontë's *Wuthering Heights*]

7. *Both Desire and Come Together.*

"Fancy that we are here!" she said, looking down at him. He was lying watching her, stroking her breasts with his fingers, under the thin nightdress. When he was warm and smoothed out, he looked young and handsome. His eyes could look so warm. And she was fresh and young like a flower.

"I want to take this off!" he said, gathering the thin batiste nightdress and pulling it over her head. She sat there with bare shoulders and longish breasts faintly golden. He loved to make her breasts swing softly, like bells.

"You must take off your pyjamas, too," she said.

"Eh nay!"

"Yes! Yes!" she commanded.

And he took off his old cotton pyjama-jacket and pushed down the trousers. Save for his hands and wrists and face and neck he was white as milk with fine slender muscular flesh. To Connie he was suddenly piercingly beautiful again, as when she had seen him that afternoon washing himself.

Gold of sunshine touched the closed white curtains. She felt it wanted to come in. [Lawrence's *Lady Chatterley's Lover*]

You will make use of more than one type of scene, working your way to the moment the hero and heroine come together in mutual trust and understanding. Direct handling of your sex scenes is not only difficult to do with delicacy but also unappealing. Indirect writing, using imagery such as symbolism and metaphor, understatement, and appealing to the senses, will arouse your readers and make your scenes believable.

D. H. Lawrence makes a statement about the importance of love over mere desire. Mellors, the former gamekeeper in *Lady Chatterley's Lover,* is writing to Connie while they are separated:

"So I love chastity now, because it is the peace that comes of fucking. I love being chaste now. I love it as snowdrops love the snow. I love this chastity, which is the pause of peace of our fucking, between us now like a snowdrop of forked white fire. And when the real spring comes, when the drawing together comes, then we can fuck the little flame brilliant and yellow, brilliant. But not now, not yet!"

X

Creating Suspense

I F you plan to write romantic suspense or Gothic novels, you will need to practice a variety of techniques to gain dramatic tension. Your reader must constantly be thinking: What will happen next? Why is the character doing that? If she could only know what I know! Doesn't she know *that* is the wrong thing to do?

Thomas Hardy, who wrote of unrequited love, was a master at using all techniques necessary to build tension. His *The Return of the Native* is a novel you should study to learn how to create suspense.

Suspense Through Setting

Just as Emily Brontë in *Wuthering Heights* raised the importance of setting, making it one of the dramatic elements in her story by paralleling the passionate relationship of the lovers Heathcliff and Catherine with the stormy, rugged atmosphere, so Hardy gives setting a major role in his novel. On Egdon Heath, a desolate landscape of furze and heather, we watch nature's struggle. As we observe the "Dureresque" characters on the scene, we see that those who blend with it survive; those who fight against it, as do two of the lovers, Eustacia Vye and Damon Wildeve, perish. The novel starts with the setting as if it were indeed the main character. The storm is "its lover" and the wind "its friend." Its struggles are similar to man's own. Hardy says of the heath what he might say of the heroine, Eustacia: "It had a lonely face, suggesting tragical possibilities."

Clym Yeobright's love of Egdon Heath and insistence on remaining there eventually clash with Eustacia's hatred of the heath, thereby destroying their marriage. So Egdon Heath plays a major role in plot movement and in the tension between characters. Clym says to Eustacia:

> "You are lonely here."
> "I cannot endure the heath, except in its purple season. The heath is a cruel taskmaster to me."
> "Can you say so?" he asked. "To my mind it is most exhilarating, and strengthening, and soothing. I would rather live on these hills than anywhere else in the world. . . . And there is a very curious Druidical stone just out there. . . . Do you often go to see it?"
> "I was not even aware that there existed any such curious Druidical stone. I am aware that there are boulevards in Paris."

City life beckons to Eustacia just as the heath calls to Clym.

Eustacia makes an ironic answer to Wildeve when the two meet secretly on the heath and he exclaims:

> "You hate the heath as much as ever; that I know."
> "I do," she murmured deeply. " 'Tis my cross, my misery, and will be my death!"

The setting itself, as in a Gothic novel, isolates the characters, making them seem more helpless. It is actually the monotony of heath life, not her love for either Wildeve or Clym, that is responsible for Eustacia's relationships and eventual attempt to escape.

Suspense Through Minor Characters

In Hardy's book the heath folk, common laborers, act like a Greek chorus by commenting on the actions of the leading characters and warning us about what is to come. They blend with the setting, causing the passions of the main characters to appear in high relief. Their superstitious sayings warn us of the impending doom.

When they act, they may unwittingly cause trouble, even adding to the downfall of the main characters. One gambles with Thomasin's and Clym's money, changing the course of the story. Another creates a tense moment for the reader when she makes an effigy of Eustacia and sticks pins in it.

Suspense Through Forewarning

Both the setting and the heath folk in *The Return of the Native* remind us repeatedly that something will go wrong. Foreshadowing is a device you will often use to alert the reader to the future, both in atmosphere and in dialogue.

The gloom of the heath prepares us for the gloom of Hardy's leading characters, Eustacia and Wildeve. We are told its face suggests "tragical possibilities," and we expect tragedy. One of the heath folk says of Eustacia: "She is very strange in her ways, living up there by herself . . ." and we are prepared for an unusual heroine who will be out of touch with those around her.

Characters' thoughts can also act as a forewarning. Eustacia, brooding, thinks: "A blaze of love, and extinction, was better than a lantern glimmer of the same which should last long years," and we are apprehensive about her fate—an early, tragic death.

Suspense Through Symbol

A remarkable piece of foreshadowing that is also symbolic occurs at the outset of *The Return of the Native* and makes use of the setting. Eustacia and Wildeve have a signal. Wildeve throws a pebble into the pond to let Eustacia know he has arrived for their secret meetings. Eustacia tells the boy who is helping to keep her bonfire lit on Guy Fawkes' night, " . . . if you hear a frog jump into the pond with a flounce like a stone thrown in, be sure you run and tell me, because it is a sign of rain." Throughout the story, Eustacia is often near the pond at dramatic moments such as that of her argument with Clym's mother, who forewarns: "You, Eustacia, stand on the edge of a precipice without knowing it."

At the conclusion of the story, it is raining, and Eustacia falls into the churning stream near the weir as, with Wildeve's help, she attempts to run away. The stone thrown into the pond earlier in the story was, ironically, a sign of rain and of doom. The pond itself symbolizes the fate of Eustacia and Wildeve against which they played out their secret drama.

Suspense Through Clues

Letting the reader know more than a character knows brings her into the story and makes her more concerned for that character. Since Clym, Wildeve, and Eustacia, in an effort to fulfill their needs, all lie to themselves about their feelings, we are much more aware of the impending doom than are they.

Eustacia sighed: it was no fragile maiden sigh, but a sigh which shook her like a shiver. Whenever a flash

of reason darted like an electric light upon her love
[Wildeve]—as it sometimes would—and showed his
imperfections, she shivered thus. But it was over in
a second, and she loved on. She knew that he trifled
with her; but she loved on.

Thomasin is loved by Diggory Venn, an itinerant red-
dleman. Red in color because of the dye he uses to mark
sheep, he acts like a Mephistophelean character, meddling
(though with the best of reasons) and changing the lives of
those around him. We can see that he is interfering, but
the characters cannot; and we react by wanting to speak
out. Keeping your reader knowledgeable can keep her in
suspense.

Suspense Through Character Interaction

A pattern that calls for secrecy on the part of characters
adds suspense. Hardy's story starts with Thomasin and
Wildeve's attempt to marry secretly, but Mrs. Yeobright,
Thomasin's aunt, calls off the banns. That very night,
Wildeve and Eustacia meet clandestinely. Later, the red-
dleman meets secretly in his van with Eustacia after she
has taken part in a mummers' play pretending to be a boy.
Clym marries Eustacia, and his mother hears about it in-
directly. Eustacia and Wildeve share the secret of their
love and their plan for Eustacia to escape. In fact, all the
main characters act at times in secret, thus jeopardizing
their own happiness, and causing tension on the part of the
reader.

Suspense Through Irony

An occurrence in a story is ironic when it has an outcome
contrary to what we expect. This device creates dramatic,
suspenseful moments; for instance, Hardy's heath folk
come to sing a welcome to Thomasin and Wildeve, not
knowing the two are unmarried, that the wedding has
been prevented.

When Thomasin finally does marry Wildeve, Eustacia, taking revenge on Wildeve, comes to the wedding as a mysterious stranger. At the crucial moment, she removes her veil and gives the bride away, unwittingly changing her own fate.

Wildeve unexpectedly comes into money, while Clym, who was to take Eustacia to Paris, is partially blind and must work as a furze cutter. Wildeve, thinking of Clym, murmurs, "If he were only to die." Instead, it is Wildeve who dies.

Suspense Through Mood

As you can see, in a tightly woven novel such as Hardy's, the various ways to create suspense are interwoven. So it is with the suspense of mood. As we watch the heath at different hours and seasons, and observe it on fine days and foul, we become anxious about the characters whose lives are enacted there. Constant references by the heath folk and other characters to their fate, superstitions, and the growing gloom set a tone that keeps us in a state of tension.

Humorous romances also will rise or fall upon the proper use of the preceding techniques, but the tension created in them ultimately will produce laughter rather than a sense of fear. Before you start writing, carefully work out what your techniques will be for gaining suspense.

XI

Two Classic Examples: Pamela and Rebecca

An Early Example

*P*AMELA is considered to be the first novel in the English language. Through it, Samuel Richardson paved the way for our present-day romantic genre.

As a boy, Richardson had written love letters for young ladies. When writing his novel, he again used letters, a form that helps the reader live through the heroine. Most of the letters are written by Pamela to her parents, describing how the young master of the house is reacting to her now that his mother, Pamela's former mistress, is dead.

Pamela's parents, from a middle-class background, have fallen on bad times; and Pamela has been acting as a servant girl in a wealthy household and has been favored by her mistress. Pamela has been taught to play the piano and to sing and has been given lovely clothes to wear, so that she now has the bearing of a gentlewoman. The young master offers to make a true gentlewoman of her; but though she is only fifteen, she realizes that his plan is to deprive her of her "honesty," as she calls her virtue. She writes to her parents that he has accosted her in the summerhouse:

> Now, you will say, all his wickedness appeared plainly. I struggled and trembled, and was so benumbed with terror, that I sunk down, not in a fit, and yet not myself; and I found myself in his arms, quite void of strength; and he kissed me two or three times, with frightful eagerness.—At last I burst from him, and was getting out of the summerhouse; but he held me back, and shut the door.

Pamela determines to go home. However, that is not so easy as we might today imagine. Her class situation has been altered. Moreover, she may not find work when she returns to the country. She will without doubt end up scrubbing floors or washing clothes, and ruining her lovely skin. Yet she insists in a letter to her parents:

> . . . set your hearts at rest; for although I have lived above myself for some time past, yet I can be content with rags and poverty, and bread and water, and will embrace them, rather than forfeit my good name, let who will be the tempter.

Though this protest seems hypocritical, since she does not go directly home, she probably is convinced she will be able to make the change.

Something else holds her back—her ambivalent feelings about her master. Pamela does not admit these feelings to herself. Instead, she rationalizes:

> Sometimes I thought I would leave the house and go to the next town, and wait an opportunity to get to you; but then I was at a loss to resolve whether to take away the things he had given me or no, and how to take them away. . . .

Pamela does what the later Gothic heroines were fond of doing: she puts herself in a position of danger. That she need not be in such danger does not occur to her, nor does it spoil the story.

We find Pamela saying the very things we should love to say. She is saucy with her master, within the bounds of eighteenth-century conversation, and the more pert she is, the more she fascinates him. After being discharged, Pamela says to her master:

> "Why, if I have done amiss, am I not left to be discharged by your housekeeper, as the other maids have been? And if Jane, or Rachel, or Hannah, were to offend, would your honour stoop to take notice of them?"

The heroine's standing up to the hero and thereby intriguing him is a key element in category romances.

Since nothing works on the master's part to win her, he decides to try rape. He hides in Pamela's closet as she and Mrs. Jervis, the housekeeper, go to bed. When he rushes out, Pamela is not beyond noticing that he is wearing "a rich silk and silver morning gown."

> Instantly, he came to the bed, (for I had crept into it, to Mrs. Jervis, with my coat on, and my shoes) and taking me in his arms, said—"Mrs. Jervis, rise, and just step up the stairs to keep the maids from coming down at this noise."

Mrs. Jervis refuses to leave, but her presence does not stop the master.

> I found his hand in my bosom, and when my fright let me know it, I was ready to die; and I sighed and screamed, and fainted away.

Pamela's timely fainting spells save her from some unfortunate situations. Since modern girls do not faint so readily, the modern author must resort to other means to free the heroine.

What the hero heard while hiding in the closet convinces him that Pamela is more worthy than any lady in the world. Nevertheless, marriage is not in his mind, for he cannot lower himself so much. He only wants her all the more. However, his pride will not let him "descend all at once," as he puts it.

Thinking she is being taken home by carriage, Pamela is instead taken to the master's country estate where she is held prisoner by yet another housekeeper, Mrs. Jewkes, by far an uglier character than Mrs. Jervis, who was fond of Pamela, so there is heightened suspense. The master dresses up as the maid and sits in the bedroom as if asleep. Before getting into bed, Pamela checks the closets as she has done each night since the last attempted rape.

> So I looked into the closet, and kneeled down in my own, as I used to do, to say my prayers, and this with my underclothes in my hand, all undressed; and passed by the poor sleeping wench, as I thought, in my return. But, oh! little did I think it was my wicked, wicked master, in a gown and petticoat of hers, and her apron over his face and shoulders.

Pamela gets into bed, and the master jumps in and kisses her with "frightful vehemence." Mrs. Jewkes holds one of Pamela's hands, encouraging him, while he holds the other, and it would seem Pamela is now lost. However, you guessed it,

> . . . I fainted away quite, and did not come to myself soon; so that they both, from the cold sweats that I was in, thought me dying.

The master continually complains of Pamela's writing so much, and steals her letters; yet it is those very letters which, ironically, save her relationship with him and with his sister, for the letters prove what a virtuous, lovely girl she is.

Though areas of the story, particularly the conclusion, depart from the typical romance pattern, you can readily see how much we are indebted to Richardson. The novel in its own time was a great success and proved to other writers that ladies in distress because of love present a very moving subject. The focus in *Pamela*, as in the contemporary romance, is on a single situation, expanding it and showing it from all sides.

The hero's problem is, should he lower himself to take this servant girl in marriage? The heroine's problem is indecision. Should she remain and finish sewing his waistcoat? Should she escape from the country estate? And behind the indecision are her ambivalent feelings for the hero. Her spunky attitude, exhibited by her continuing to write, to plan escapes, and to stand up for herself, helps Pamela to rise in the world by becoming the master's wife.

A Recent Example

A contemporary novel which has helped to set the pattern for the popular romance is Daphne du Maurier's *Rebecca* (Doubleday). Its heroine, the narrator, is unmarried. The first person of the story, she lacks a name. She is young and parentless, acting as a companion to Mrs. Van Hopper, a gauche middle-aged American woman visiting Monte Carlo. The girl meets Maxim de Winter, who, Mrs. Van Hopper tells her, is mourning the death of his wife. Maxim de Winter seems to take pity on the girl when Mrs. Van Hopper is ill. " 'You know,' he said, 'we've got a bond in common, you and I. We are both alone in the world.' "

Both hero and heroine are described very early:

He belonged to a walled city of the fifteenth century, a city of narrow, cobbled streets, and thin spires, where the inhabitants wore pointed shoes and worsted hose. His face was arresting, sensitive, medieval in some strange inexplicable way, and I was reminded of a portrait seen in a gallery I had forgotten where, of a certain Gentleman Unknown. Could one but rob him of his English tweeds, and put him in black, with lace at his throat and wrists, he would stare down at us in our new world from a long distant past—a past where men walked cloaked at night, and stood in the shadow of old doorways, a past of narrow stairways and dim dungeons, a past of whispers in the dark, of shimmering rapier blades, of silent, exquisite courtesy.

It is with this hero that the young, shy heroine of a much lower class falls in love. And it is just such description that lends the novel a Gothic air. Though the heroine is not ambivalent about her feelings and does not continually place herself in danger from the hero, some of the ghostly trappings will be present once the scene shifts to Manderley, the hero's manor house.

Meanwhile, the hero is quick to see the heroine's embarrassment at Mrs. Van Hopper's remarks and shows a kindness in attempting to put her at ease:

I think he realized my distress, for he leant forward in his chair and spoke to me, his voice gentle, asking if I would have more coffee, and when I refused and shook my head I felt that his eyes were still upon me, puzzled, reflective.

Repeated kindnesses win her to a quick promise to marry him. It is easy to see he has made her feel worthwhile. After their first outing she writes:

I was a person of importance, I was grown up at last. That girl, who, tortured by shyness, would stand outside the sitting-room door twisting a handkerchief in her hands, while from within came that babble of confused chatter so unnerving to the intruder—she had gone with the wind that afternoon. She was a poor creature, and I thought of her with scorn if I considered her at all.

And so the two love. But it is not the typical genre love

of happiness ever after. Instead, we start with a marriage
and a warning:

> I am glad it cannot happen twice, the fever of first
> love. For it is a fever, and a burden, too, whatever
> the poets may say. They are not brave, the days when
> we are twenty-one. They are full of little cowardices,
> little fears without foundation, and one is so easily
> bruised, so swiftly wounded, one falls to the first
> barbed word.

Hers is not the quick, spunky reaction of the American,
more aggressive heroine. Hers is a deep courage and
strength, hidden by timidity. This lack of identity, this
definition of self in the context of a distressful love situation, has been a model for modern Harlequin Romance
and Gothic heroines. As the story gathers force, the heroine's strength is tested and retested, and she very gradually
grows before our eyes. What never wavers is her love for
Maxim.

When they marry and move to Manderley, his beloved
English manor house, the ghost of Rebecca, his first wife,
influences the actions of all the others. Manderley itself is
a ghost, for when the story opens, it is no more. Its specter
and its specter mistress dominate an eerie tale and become
tangible, while the actual mistress, the second Mrs. de
Winter, is almost wraithlike until she learns to show her
strength. *Rebecca* is an ideal book through which to study
character revelation.

Maxim, too, is a model character in that he is silent,
but not because he is boring or bored. Rather, he is complex, feeling deeply but hiding his true thoughts and emotions. Through his actions, one is led to believe that this
truly has been a marriage of convenience. It is the heroine's
tenacity—a good trait to remember for your own heroines—that helps to save him and that saves the marriage.

Great romances exhibit strong characterization and intriguing plot convolutions. If you wish to write well, the

finest teachers are the classic stories themselves. Buy paperbacks and colored pens, and get in the habit of marking every romance you read. If a passage doesn't work, write a note to yourself in the margin. If it does work, mention why. Being aware of how authors handle their problems is the surest way of making wise choices yourself.

XII

The Regency Romance

R EGENCY novels are unique in that they are novels of manners; they take place against a limited backdrop, the English social scene in the second decade of the nineteenth century; and they are written in the language of the period. Society of that time concerned itself with fashion and manners more than with social justice. Such a society lends itself to satire.

Backdrop

Backdrop is the first defining element of a Regency romance. The action takes place in a nine-year period, 1811–1820, and the Regency writer must study this period thoroughly. The early nineteenth century is known under three names: the Romantic, the Gothic, and the Regency period. Modern Regency novels deal with society under the prince regent, the future George IV, who was given the ruling power when George III was proclaimed mad.

That son loved a life of pleasure; and the social scene, in London in winter months and at Brighton by the sea in the summer, was a lively one. These years were a time of unrest for England. The industrial, middle class was ever on the rise and would eventually diminish the aristocracy. Great changes were taking place in transportation. England had lost the American colonies under George III and was now fighting Napoleon. Though the upper classes for the most part ignored the war, paying mercenaries to fight it, the social order was changing rapidly, never again to be the same. The obvious answer, especially under a prince who loved the social scene, was to seize the day. And the wealthy and titled did just that.

Society

A small group of society women set themselves up as arbiters of Society with a capital *S*. They formed a club called Almack's and held a dance every Wednesday night. By some accounts, the affairs were not so elegant. Some complained the rooms were barnlike and the bread and butter or cake sometimes stale. Nevertheless, the right people were there. It became socially imperative, whether male or female, to receive a voucher, an entrance card, to Almack's. Young ladies' hearts were broken and careers destroyed when no voucher was forthcoming.

This was a time of strict social rules. Moral rules were left to the middle class to follow. These rules may be one reason the contemporary reader enjoys returning to this period. In an age when we have few guidelines, we can appreciate going back to a time when most of life's events were prescribed, from the fashionable time to ride in Hyde Park (five to six each evening) to when a young lady might be seen on St. James Street (in the morning, when accompanied by a maid or footman, and in the afternoon, never).

In a modern Regency novel the heroine follows the middle-class rules of propriety. Usually a kiss is as far as her relations with the hero will go, and this kiss comes rather late in the story. There may be several kisses, but society does not permit more. In true Regency society, the girl was expected to be a virgin before marriage, but the rules surrounding her courtship were made more for social than for moral reasons. Marriages were for convenience, to align wealth and title; so her husband would keep his mistress or take a new one. His wife was expected to have an heir or sometimes two in order to continue the family line. After that, she could take her *cicisbeo* (lover), and no questions would be asked about the father of future offspring. That some of the children resembled other men was tittered about but accepted.

For the contemporary Regency formula, the man must be wealthier than the heroine, though she may have money.

Clothes were especially important to both men and women of the period. Evening gowns had low necks so that jewels could be displayed. It is ironic that we repeatedly return to a time when women were treated like horses, and both were used to display a man's wealth. The Cyprian dressed as expensively as the wife, for she was actually a courtesan, often with a lively mind, with whom the man had something in common. She had her box at the opera where she was joined by her admirers, entertaining them openly.

The arbiter of fashion for men's wear was Beau Brummel. The son of a clerk, he rose in society by his wit. He preferred subdued colors, though some dandies wore brightly embroidered vests and the fashionable colors of the day such as bottle green or primrose. High starched collars were in vogue, and the knot of the necktie was of extreme importance, rather like the roll of an Englishman's umbrella today. Men also wore padded shoulders; and the wasp waist, ever popular for Regency heroes, was achieved by wearing a Cumberland corset. If you write a Regency romance, it is best to eliminate the corset for the hero, who would, of course, never need one.

Amusements

The favorite amusement of the period was conversation. Anyone who was a wit, though he lacked the proper background, could move to the top of society. Henry Luttrell, who was the illegitimate son of a gardener's daughter and an Irish peer, was a great favorite because of his wit. One was also admired if he could entertain by being the subject of gossip. Lord Byron and Lady Caroline Lamb were adored as long as their spicy affair was delighting the social scene. However, boundaries existed, and when rumors of Byron's incest with his half-sister reached society, he was ostracized from the polite world.

Card playing was another favorite activity. Women played as well as men, but the men often played at their clubs, gaming until the wee hours. In *The Reluctant Duke*, Julia baffles the hero by continually beating him at cards. In fact, a card game and the wager involved are used as a plot device for the story.

Both sexes rode, and horses were a favorite topic. Tattersalls was the spot to purchase a horse. Carriage riding was also popular as well as necessary, and hunting in the country was the fashion.

Men favored boxing at Jackson's. Women were expected to play the piano or harp, sing, and draw or paint. Dancing was a favorite with both sexes. The lively Countess Lieven introduced a dance so shocking a young lady had to have the permission of one of the ladies of Almack's to first dance it, even in her own home. It was called lascivious, and it was named the waltz.

Food

In a period piece, be sure to describe how the food was served. In Regency England, the idea of courses was just coming in from France, and the English did not favor it. Though they did have more than one course, they tended to mix all types of food together. Platters were not passed around the table. Instead, guests were to take a sampling of the variety in front of them. If someone wanted a dish from another spot at the table, he would send a servant to fetch it. Both on his plate and on his fork, the diner would combine any number of foods we would not mix today, such as quail, jellied eel, and pineapple in cream. Numerous dishes were placed on the table, but one was not expected to eat all types of food offered. The kitchens were a long way from the dining hall, so the food would be lukewarm at best.

In a Regency novel, we are concerned with the wealthy. The poor of Regency England were in very sad straits. But we close our eyes, as did the society of the time, to "flash houses" where at an early age boys were taught to be thieves and girls to be prostitutes. We ignore the poor who lived in the country, often dining on rancid bread and rotten potatoes. And we ignore the children forced to hard labor. There was a keen observer of these sufferings, a boy who grew up in the Regency period and was dramatically influenced by it—Charles Dickens. Later he was to attack these evils. For our part, we are telling a love story, a fantasy in a glamorous setting, and we must stick to our task.

Language

Language is the second defining element of the Regency period. Since, in a novel of manners, words take precedence over actions, nuances of speech convey the characters' true selves.

Polite words are essential in a polite society. A villain can lurk behind polite words. A fool will usually misuse the words. Though characters may be open and expressive, such as Elizabeth in *Pride and Prejudice,* all remarks are made within the limits of a prescribed language and social custom. Verbal expression shows the degree of refinement.

In a Regency novel, a character's speech definitely places him or her within the social structure.

Since Regency romances take place in the British Isles, the phrasing must be British. Furthermore, the language must be nineteenth-century in tone. A period with formalized manners is one with polite phrases of speech. If a Regency miss likes a man, she says, "I find him excessively agreeable," or, "He has great delicacy of mind." If she dislikes him, she says, "He lacks conversation"—quite a mark against one when we consider that conversation was the main amusement of the day—or she may say, "He is nothing but pride and consequence." Remarks dealing with her inner feelings take on a formal tone.

The language must suit the character. We can study its use in the papers, diaries, journals, novels, and plays of the period. Regency aristocrats sometimes affect usages such as "don't" for "doesn't." Young dandies use a great deal of slang. Today we might call someone a fool. In the Regency period we call him a *noddy*, a *pea-goose*, a *ninny*, or a *dolt*, or we might say he is *caper-witted, idiotish, queer in the attic, touched in the upper works, skitter-witted*, or *addle-brained*. If someone is talking nonsense, he is talking *gammon, flummery, skimble-skamble*, or *bibble-babble*. Throwing in the odd phrase without carefully working on the speech patterns for a period piece mars many romances.

The Comedy of Manners

The comedy of manners is the third defining element of the period. Congreve in the seventeenth century, Goldsmith and Sheridan in the eighteenth, as well as Wilde in the nineteenth century, practiced a form of realistic comedy that points out the foibles of artificial types in society. These plays are graceful, witty, and intellectual; mainly they are humorously critical. In a comedy of manners, as they are called, a pair of attractive lovers, the girl as bright and as witty as the young man, gracefully and cynically banter their way toward a romantic union. Their dialogue is actually more important than the plot. Two comedies of manners to peruse are Oliver Goldsmith's *She Stoops to Conquer* and Richard Sheridan's *The Rivals*.

The Novel of Manners

Jane Austen's novels of the early nineteenth century follow in the tradition of the comedy of manners by giving us heroines who are the equal of the heroes and by humorously criticizing society and its sentimentality through the lovers. Much as do Goldsmith and Sheridan, Austen works on a small scale, examining the daily lives of the landed gentry. The stories belong to the heroines, and each heroine's main problem is the choice of a husband. On that choice depends her future social position and income. The choice is not an easy one. Often the wrong man appears desirable. That the heroine picks the right man reveals her basic strength of character, which allows her to mature and make the correct decision.

Austen's novels of manners differ from the comedies of manners in that her characters are well defined rather than stereotypes. Her irony, though present, is subtle and gentle, not pointed.

In *Pride and Prejudice,* we see the Bennet family, made up of a foolish, shallow mother, a caustic father, and five daughters for whom husbands must be found. The portrayal of the two elder Bennets, in a bad marriage and searching out five husbands so that their daughters can enter the same precarious institution, is ironic. Inside drawing rooms, the fates of the lovers are decided. A young lady's future security depends on the match, so her marriage is not only a necessity but also a social matter, changing the fortunes of others in the family. Therefore, all parties involve themselves in a possible union. Austen is able to focus on this turning point in her characters' lives and find high drama.

The heroine and hero of the novel, Elizabeth Bennet and the aristocratic Mr. Darcy, are models for today's romance writer. When they first meet, they clash; but their wit and strength of character cause them to be interested in each other. Both attractive, they make a good pair, though their personalities at first separate them. Mr. Darcy scorns the lack of refinement he sees in some of the Bennets; Elizabeth, because of their first meeting and later out of loyalty to family, sees Mr. Darcy as a snob. She says to him:

". . . *your* defect is a propensity to hate everybody."
"And yours," he replied with a smile, "is wilfully to misunderstand them."

Elizabeth is charming, witty, and spunky, but is easily prejudiced against the haughty Mr. Darcy. Darcy, on his part, is prejudiced against the entire middle class; yet he is impressed as Elizabeth stands up to him.

Both characters grow. Elizabeth must face her impetuosity and Darcy must accept her family. We find he is not proud in all areas but sensitive and generous and complex, deeper than we at first suspected.

Twentieth-century authors depicting the Regency period tend to follow Austen's lead and adopt a humorous, gently critical approach. The heroine is equal to the man, and the banter of the two is often amusing as well as ironic. The girl is not usually as submissive to the hero as are some heroines of other types of romances, and she doesn't necessarily think of his wishes in performing an action.

A Modern Regency Novel

Georgette Heyer is the best-known modern Regency writer. She is particularly skillful at plotting and is accurate in depicting the period and in her use of language. She sometimes includes a tinge of mystery in her Regency plots.

In *Cousin Kate,* Kate at twenty-four has lost both parents and goes to live on the estate of her father's half-sister, Lady Broome. The latter achieved her ambition by marrying Sir Timothy and now glories in her role as the mistress of Staplewood. She is more than kind to Kate, heaping gifts upon her and encouraging Kate to befriend Torquil, the beautiful nineteen-year-old son, who is treated as if he were still a child.

We do not even hear about the hero, Philip Broome, for several chapters and do not meet him until well into the story. However, in this case the way must be prepared so that Kate becomes angry with him at first sight. Now the usual hero-heroine conflict can go on, each readily misunderstanding the other. He is sarcastic and aloof, but she must finally admit to herself that although there is no reason why she should like him, ". . . she had formed a decided partiality for Mr. Philip Broome."

Kate becomes very bored at Staplewood. Torquil is bored; Philip is bored. It is a story worth reading to see how an author can present a boring scene without making the reader yawn.

First, the setting takes on the feeling of a prison. Kate finds that she is locked in at night, discovering this after hearing a cry of terror in the night. Hints are dropped about Torquil's strange behavior. Later, Kate finds a dead rabbit after hearing a human scream. The animal has been removed from the snare that trapped it, and its head has been torn off. Then Torquil almost shoots Kate in an attempt to shoot a harmless dog.

Kate has not heard from her old abigail (lady's maid), and the reader knows that letters have been intercepted, that Kate is more marooned than she has realized.

Lady Broome is a well-drawn character, causing Kate to feel she is "enclosed in a silken net." A simple scene in which Lady Broome peels an apple for her son, who does not want to eat, not only describes her but also is shocking as it reveals the almost diabolical control she is able to exert while appearing sweet and charming:

"There, Torquil! I haven't lost my old skill!" She showed him an unbroken spiral of apple-peel, and turned her head to tell Kate that when he had been a little boy he had eaten apples only for the joy of watching her peel them for him. "As he will do today!" she said, cutting the fruit into neat quarters, and arranging them on a plate.

Torquil once again is humiliated.

Lady Broome eventually tells Kate that she expects her to marry Torquil, and Kate realizes that

. . . by marrying Torquil to her own niece she might hope to keep him in subjection, and to continue to reign at Staplewood after Sir Timothy's death.

Penniless and owing everything to Lady Broome, Kate is suspected by Philip of being after the Staplewood fortune. Naturally, all comes right in the end, but the note of mystery keeps the story well-paced.

Research is the key to approaching the Regency period. (See Chapter 20, "Accurate Research.") Time spent mentally living in that span of years, and noting the various levels of society and of acceptable behavior, will result in more salable Regency novels.

XIII

The Romantic Suspense or Gothic Novel

WRITERS tend to approach romantic suspense in one of two ways. Either they do a type of detective story in which the heroine is the amateur sleuth, picking up clues to a problem as a background to romance, or they add actual horror, creating a Gothic. Many use the terms *Gothic* and *romantic suspense* interchangeably. In this book I shall make a slight distinction between the two terms for clarity's sake.

The Gothic Romance

The early Gothics of the eighteenth and nineteenth centuries were concerned with terror and were derived from folklore. Just as Gothic arches and the rustic in nature were supposed to help the mind transcend the mundane, terror, too, was expected to fulfill this purpose.

A popular early Gothic tale is Horace Walpole's *The

Castle of Otronto, 1764 (Dover Publications). In this story, a giant helmet falls from the sky, crushing the young prince who is about to be married. Portraits move, a statue bleeds, disjointed arms and legs are seen. Amidst all this there is a contrived story of an evil prince, Manfred, who lusts for his dead son's bride-to-be and wants to have his own marriage to a wife of many years annulled. His daughter, Isabella, is infatuated with a peasant youth, Theodore, who, rather than Manfred, turns out to be the real heir to the title. Theodore is also a look-alike to the dead Alonso, the original owner of the castle. The elements of horror play a major part in determining the outcome of the story. Alonso's ghost appears as a giant, destroying the castle and revealing Theodore as heir. Isabella and Theodore then marry. The characters are more or less left to the fate intended for them rather than working out problems for themselves.

In Ann Radcliffe's *The Mysteries of Udolpho,* 1794, Emily St. Aubert is forcefully taken from the man she loves, Valancourt, by her guardian and uncle by marriage, Montoni. Thinking to obtain both Emily's and his wife's properties, Montoni takes her to a Gothic castle, Udolpho, in the Apennines. There Emily fears the attentions of Count Morano, whom Montoni has until now wished her to marry. Besides her never-ending fear of the count, Emily must suffer from terrifying moments caused by the horror of the setting. Castle Udolpho has since served as the model for all Gothic backgrounds.

> Emily gazed with melancholy awe upon the castle, which she understood to be Montoni's. . . . Silent, lonely and sublime, it seemed to stand the sovereign of the scene, and to frown defiance on all, who dared to invade its solitary reign. As the twilight deepened, its features became more awful in obscurity, and Emily continued to gaze, till its clustering towers were alone seen, rising over the tops of the woods, beneath whose thick shade the carriages soon after began to ascend.

Udolpho, ancient and crumbling, has long, drafty galleries, haunted rooms, and secret passageways. One such passage leads to Emily's room, which is in a remote part of the castle. This passage deservedly causes Emily much alarm. Fearful sights include lights in passageways, blood on the steps of the turret, an apparent specter, and a dead body.

Throughout her experiences, Emily remains courageous and sympathetic to the needs of even her enemies. Her bravery is set in contrast to the fear of her aunt's serving girl, Annette. Emily consistently exhibits the Gothic mentality:

> . . . a terror of this nature, as it occupies and expands the mind, and elevates it to high expectation, is purely sublime, and leads us, by a kind of fascination, to seek even the object, from which we appear to shrink.

It is the strength of Emily's resolution that conquers her fear, yet the gloom of the castle repeatedly reawakens terror.

Emily's greatest torment is that she is parted from her love, Valancourt. Seclusion in the castle makes the parting seem final and the love hopeless.

The villainous characters in this tale exhibit rage and jealousy and vengeance, whereas Emily always shows pity and a consciousness of her duty. Whatever the situation, and though she may seem meek, she has what her enemies lack: a sense of her own worth. This inner strength gives her the courage to stand up for what she considers to be right.

Emily also has determination. We are told that "the strength of her resolution remedied the weakness of her frame." This comment could be made about all romantic heroines.

Eventually, the mysterious happenings are given logical explanations. These do not reduce the mood, which remains a haunting one few have matched.

Romances with Gothic Elements

Though they did not write true Gothics, the three Brontë sisters brought many Gothic elements into their Victorian romances, and their books serve as models of what we to-day call Gothic. In *Jane Eyre,* 1847, by Charlotte Brontë, the title character is the sort of plain, submissive girl we see later in *Rebecca* and, like the second Mrs. de Winter, she has a great deal of hidden courage that must blossom gradually. The heroine's childhood years and the later episodes with St. John Rivers and his sisters are Victorian and not in the least Gothic. However, the love story between Mr. Rochester and Jane is Gothic at its best.

Jane applies for a position as governess and is accepted at Thornfield Hall, the Rochester estate. There she learns to know and love her master. He is a singular person, not handsome but virile; and he has flaws. Yet as Jane gets to know him, he grows better-looking to her. This change lets us know how deeply she is affected:

> And was Mr. Rochester now ugly in my eyes? No, reader: gratitude, and many associations, all pleasurable and genial, made his face the object I best liked to see; his presence in a room was more cheering than the brightest fire. Yet I had not forgotten his faults: indeed, I could not, for he brought them frequently before me. He was proud, sardonic, harsh to inferiority of every description; in my secret soul I knew that his great kindness to me was balanced by unjust severity to many others. He was moody, too; unaccountably so.

Jane later says, "I thought there were excellent materials in him; though for the present they hung together somewhat spoiled and tangled." Such comments make Rochester seem more human than is the hero of the formula romance.

Other women who surpass Jane in wealth and social accomplishments are on the scene, as they are in the contemporary romances; but Jane, as do her modern counterparts, surpasses them in depth of character and ability to truly love. And—shades of *Pamela*—Mr. Rochester disguises himself as a woman. In this instance, he dresses as a gypsy fortune-teller to test Jane's love for him.

Jane, like Emily in *The Mysteries of Udolpho,* has a singleness of purpose that sustains her when she is away from Thornfield and that takes her back to Mr. Rochester to support him in his crisis. These are inflexible heroines who do not waver in their purpose. What could be a weakness gives them courage to do what is necessary. In each heroine, juxtaposed with inflexibility and common sense, is a passionate nature. The combination of disparate qualities makes them attractive heroines. A weakness in many category romance heroines is that they have only one character trait.

Thornfield is the huge old manor house of the Gothics. Within is a mysterious character whom Jane is told is Mrs. Poole. A ghostlike person, Mrs. Poole walks at night, once almost killing Mr. Rochester. Later, she tries on the wedding veil the night before Jane's wedding. Jane describes the creature to Mr. Rochester:

> ". . . oh, sir, I never saw a face like it! It was a discoloured face—it was a savage face. I wish I could forget the roll of the red eyes and the fearful blackened inflation of the lineaments!"

Jane goes on to describe its actions:

> "It drew aside the window-curtain and looked out: perhaps it saw dawn approaching, for, taking the candle, it retreated to the door. Just at my bedside, the figure stopped: the fiery eye glared upon me—she thrust up her candle close to my face, and extinguished it under my eyes. I was aware her lurid visage flamed over mine, and I lost consciousness: for the second time in my life—only the second time—I became insensible from terror."

This figure has earlier set fire to Mr. Rochester's room, almost killing him before he is awakened by Jane. The sturdy old chestnut tree is split by lightning, forewarning catastrophe. Finally, his wife sets fire to Thornfield Hall, and Mr. Rochester is blinded and maimed in trying to save her. We learn the truth about his mad wife. He has been punished for attempting to marry Jane while his wife is still living.

The tale has true Gothic trappings—a gloomy manor house, an evil, terrifying figure, and mystery. Against these, Charlotte Brontë places a moving love story about two people who overlook flaws in each other and grow together to share an unshakable love.

A book that is not as well known, *The Tenant of Wildfell Hall,* 1848, by Anne Brontë, makes use of a mysterious old mansion and a mysterious woman who has come to stay in it. The first person of the tale is a young man who is infatuated with this woman. As he tries to untangle the mystery surrounding her, he falls deeply in love with her. The terror in this story is the woman's. She fears the actions of her unpredictable husband. This novel, too, is a Victorian romance with some Gothic elements woven in, and is best described as mysterious. Again, a deep love between characters gradually grows.

The heroine, Mrs. Huntingdon, deserves some study. She has the courage to take her son and leave her husband because of the latter's unseemly behavior. She thereby acts against the social customs of the day and the wishes of her own brother. She then sets out to earn her own living by painting pictures. However, when she is needed, she has the strength to return to nurse her sick husband until his death. She finally relates romantically to the narrator of the tale, who has long loved her. She is far more compatible with this man than she had been with the conventional hero-type that she had first married. A modern heroine, ahead of her time, Mrs. Huntingdon should be of special interest to those writing contemporary romances.

Wuthering Heights, by Emily Brontë, becomes a symbolic story of love. It, too, has Gothic trappings—the mood of terror and gloom, the strange house called Wuthering Heights (*wuthering* meaning stormy), the apparition of

Catherine Henshaw, and Heathcliff's longings that follow Catherine beyond the grave. But again, this is a Victorian romance rather than a terror story, and the heroine is not ennobled by her experience.

Catherine, who has courage and vitality, is enchanted with the glamorous world of the neighboring Thrushcross Grange, and the swarthy and morose Heathcliff is attempting to hold onto a lover who is eluding him. They act as original, complex models for today's romance writers. However, their passion takes them far beyond the attraction of chemistry, beyond even a workable relationship in life. Catherine and Heathcliff cannot find a balance between opposing desires. Catherine must perish; Heathcliff must live to suffer.

The Modern Gothic Formula

The modern Gothic formula brings the heroine onto the scene just when events are coming to a head for other characters. She then is a catalyst for the others, accelerating changes already taking place.

Mood is the most important element of a Gothic. Your use of funereal terms (*death, ghostly, pale, grave*) and your pacing will help you to achieve a terrifying effect. Your setting will be frightening, and you will repeatedly foreshadow doom for the heroine. You may have characters murdered and the heroine's life threatened, but murders take place offstage. You are not concerned with the actual murder. In fact, to add mystery, murder attempts may be made to look like accidents. Nor are you involved with solving a crime. Your trappings will be used to create a terrifying backdrop which will reveal your heroine's character.

Supernatural forces may threaten the heroine. That these are explained away in time makes them no less effective. Use of true occult in a Gothic depends upon current publishing trends.

Two leading men are usually involved; one is an antihero. The real hero, as you know, is brooding and looks as if he were the one bringing about all the trouble. The villain usually appears cheerful and kind.

At first, upsetting events may keep the lovers suspicious of each other and apart. Eventually, the two will come together, their passions heightened by the sharing of strange experiences. Emotional as the lovers may be, you will not involve them in explicit sex, since you will be unweaving the web of mystery you have spun so carefully.

Victoria Holt shows a fine hand at working with emotions and terror. In *Shivering Sands* (Doubleday), she uses nocturnal ghostly lights, which are later explained, and then ends with real quicksand, a horror that need not be explained away. In *The Legend of the Seventh Virgin* (Doubleday), the author combines Cornish superstitions, a mysterious mansion, a girl whose grandmother has a witch's knowledge of herbs, and a strange legend in which the seventh virgin is walled up alive. In Holt's tales the element of terror is stronger than that of mystery. Yet the frightening things do have logical explanations, as they do in Radcliffe's stories.

The Romantic Suspense Story

Phyllis A. Whitney is particularly adept at the romantic suspense story, a term she uses interchangeably with Gothic; but in her stories, unraveling the mystery takes precedence over horrifying elements. In *The Golden Unicorn* (Doubleday), Courtney Marsh, a well-known reporter, is searching for her natural parents, her adoptive parents having died. Her search leads her, quite plausibly, to the Shingles, a mansion on the coast of Long Island, to interview the famous artist Judith Rhodes. A newspaper clipping among the papers of Courtney's adoptive parents shows a painting by Miss Rhodes. In it there is an outline of a cloud in the shape of a unicorn, and in the margin are penciled the words, "Is this the unicorn in our Courtney's life?" A clue. Another clue is the golden unicorn that was around Courtney's neck when she was adopted as a baby.

Courtney meets a strange family at the Shingles, one she would just as soon not belong to. She also meets danger and some threats to her life, since she enters a stage already set. Eventually there is a murder. Finally, Courtney herself for a third time escapes death.

In a romantic suspense story, near-murders replace the near-rapes of the historical romances. The heroine need not be in these situations, so the writer explains her involvement by making her curious and anxious about some problem or desirous of helping someone else. However, if a weak spot is going to appear, it will be in the heroine's insistence on putting herself in danger.

Points to Remember

The main thing to keep in mind while working with this formula is to create a heroine with courage. Never let her spirit flag, even when she's frightened; and never make her too passive. She is the acting force. That action, aroused by curiosity, will take her to any number of places where she will meet real danger.

The second point to remember is to create a frightening mood. Now is the time to use your skill in making the reader feel the desolation of the scene. Your heroine will hear strange sounds and see startling sights. She will be aware of a feeling of doom hanging over the ghostly setting night and day. The setting need not be a manor house, and the story need not take place in the past. The mood and the emotional conflicts can lend themselves to a variety of settings.

If you enjoy mystery and moods and unraveling problems, the Gothic or romantic suspense is for you.

XIV

The Gay Romance

T HE formula romance changes very little when written for a homosexual audience, whether male or female. In lesbian romances, the "older woman" is like the hero of the heterosexual romances. In the male stories, the "mistress" of the story has many female qualities.

The Formula

A typical homosexual romance shows a young man in his late teens or early twenties, somewhat naive, very beautiful, and cut off from his family. He finds his haven with an older man in his thirties who resembles the hero in the heterosexual novels—tall, dark, handsome, rugged, arrogant, surly, even cruel, but fascinating. The young man often appears helpless, relying very much on his older friend. The younger one is emotional; the older, apparently indifferent. Their emotions help to create misunderstandings.

Sex scenes in the homosexual romance are treated as they are in most romances: sensuously rather than explicitly. Other than some kisses and petting, movements are usually hinted at rather than given in detail. The lovers' emotional reactions are paramount. Though the hero is remote and the young man ambivalent, the hero is good to the young man, in many situations putting him at ease. Gradually, true love grows, and the two come together for lasting happiness.

Two Formula Romances

Vincent Virga in *Gaywick* (Avon) has set his romance in New York, mainly the South Shore of Long Island, in the early twentieth century. Much of the action takes place in a remote manor house, surrounded by mystery. On the cover of the novel is the usual Gothic mansion with one light in the window and desolate-looking characters waiting pensively by a raging sea. This cover differs from the covers of the women's romances only in that it shows a tall, dark hero, his hand on the shoulder of a blond young man. Within the covers is a fine example of what a Gothic should be.

Robert, a small ash-blond boy with large green eyes and pellucid skin, loses his father to death and his mother to madness. He goes to live as a librarian on the estate of the financially successful Donough Gaylord, who at thirty is, ironically, New York's most eligible bachelor. Told in the first person, the story immediately involves the reader with the precocious, extremely sensitive youth. His father, a high school principal, was responsible for his education, and the boy is well schooled in the classics. He is also ready intellectually, though not emotionally, for the sophisticated world he enters at Gaywick, the manor house on Long Island.

Virga appeals constantly to the senses so that even a blanket in the carriage that Robert takes to his destination is of the softest cashmere. We are prepared for the opulence to come. We are also forewarned about a possible blight on the scene when we are told that the monogrammed *G* on the blanket is black and embraces Robert's legs "like some great spider."

The setting of Donough Gaylord's town house, where Robert is first interviewed, is lavish. Before he meets Donough, Robert's heart pounds "in trepidation" and his senses "quicken." When he meets the hero, we are aware of the boy's chemical reaction:

> He is just above six feet in height, but being broad-shouldered, he gives the impression of a much taller man. His hair is like a raven's plumage. He wore formal evening attire. . . . His eyes are enormous—almond-shaped—and of the palest gray, a silver dusk on a summer's day. In their depths I recognized genuine interest, not momentary curiosity. I blushed and looked away. Then I returned his gaze, drawn by those twilight eyes.

Robert is overcome with the art collection and with the collector:

> I had risen from my shyness like a bird from a thicket, and suddenly, shocked by my boldness, unaccustomed to such freedom, I flew back to the safety of my defenses.

After an innocuous comment by Gaylord, Robert says:

> I blushed a deeper scarlet. I felt humiliated by not being able to control the suffusion.

Robert, noticing that the older man, beneath his elegant exterior, is also uncertain, feels a bond between himself and Donough. In his journal, Robert writes of platonic love. He wants to actually *be* Donough Gaylord.

Soon, Robert must leave the town house for Gaywick,

a "vast and lonely place" on Long Island. It, too, is filled with artistic treasures, one, a Cellini bronze faun. "The creature played a flute while gripping in its left hand a fistful of priapic abundance." We immediately are aware of opposing platonic and sybaritic views of sex as the author prepares us for Robert's later trials dealing with the question: What is love?

At Gaywick we are introduced to a variety of characters, many more than in the usual Gothic. And through them we meet a variety of homosexual types: the older Denvers, who becomes infatuated with and is taken advantage of by the young, immoral Jones; the loving couple, Mortimer and Goodbody, who have a law practice; the mad Keyes; and the pornographic Cormack. All show some side of sexuality that Robert, in growing, must encounter and either accept, reject, or understand.

Robert has, not a feminine temperament, but an artistic one. He has a certain strength in that he goes after what he wants and gets it. However, he is not the continually cheerful, spunky sort of which the romance heroines are made. He often falls upon the thorns of life and bleeds—and cries out. But such a supersensitive person is believable and well suited to the Gothic drama.

The central problem of this book is not, Will the lovers get together? but, Will Robert grow and find what is truly meaningful in love? The author suggests he will do the latter only by learning the true meaning of self-love: "One must strive to live *with,* not for or through." He also must learn to let instinct and reason act together as equals, neither one subservient to the other. Even Donough, the hero whom everyone looks up to, must grow and learn a parallel lesson to Robert's: self-love allows one to love another openly, without shame.

Throughout, the author combines the romance formula with techniques of good writing. We have already mentioned the strong appeal to the senses; for instance, cologne is "dry and musky, redolent of autumnal flowers." As in the women's romances, clothes are important. All the lavish outfits that Gaylord brings for Robert are described. Removing clothes is as important as in any romance.

The sex scenes are handled tastefully. In one scene, Robert and Donough are swimming:

> A wave swelled and thrust me into his arms. We laughed together. I kissed him, at first tenderly, apologizing one last time, before kissing him as I had wanted to from the moment I saw him. He frowned and looked surprised; then responded with such ardor that we were nearly taken by the current. I led him to the far, seaward end of the jetty, to the flat promontory exposed by the low tide. We did not speak until love had been answered. In each other's arms, we repudiated suffering, accepting the pleasures of loving. No longer neophyte, I knew my desires. We met as equals in the most exciting of combats. We achieved manly estate.

Suspense is important to the Gothic, and Virga builds dramatically to the climax. He is adept at using forewarning to prepare the reader. Robert hugs the cat, Cael, and whispers, "Love is my strength. Love is my only defense." He then adds to the reader, "Love was my greatest enemy." As the tension mounts, the forewarnings become more urgent.

This is a world of drug-induced nightmares, secret passageways, eerie appearances of strange faces, a mad musician—even murder. The Gothic trappings are replete; yet ghostly as they seem, all are explained eventually. To tell more would be to spoil unusual twists of plot. Suffice it to say that the epilogue is romantically satisfying.

Victoria Ramstetter, in *The Marquise and the Novice* (Naiad), has also chosen the Gothic mold to tell her tale of lesbian love. Again, the pattern works well with an older, mysterious woman, the Marquise Anneliese de Rochelle, haughty and proud, and the young, inexperienced governess, Kate, from the convent. In this story, the girl, with eyes too large for her face, is the usual Gothic heroine. In this instance, although naive, she gradually becomes aware of her lesbian leanings. Without realizing it, she is in a household of lesbians, and is frightened when she sees two servant girls kissing. Lonely and longing for a close bond with another woman, she is intrigued by what she has seen and gradually realizes she loves the marquise.

The marquise has been described almost as one would describe a romantic hero. She is tall with very large, unladylike hands and clipped nails. She sprawls on chairs as would a young lord and always rides in riding pants, straddling the horse, rather than sidesaddle, wearing a long skirt. Her clothes are cut to show off her body and make her look handsome. As do the romantic heroes, the marquise smiles crookedly and is nonchalant, causing the heroine to feel shy. In this case, the heroine is both attracted and repelled, exhibiting the usual ambivalence; only in this instance, she does not understand her own sexuality. She does know that the idea of marriage is repugnant to her.

As Kate becomes ever more fascinated with the marquise, she becomes more beautiful herself. But Kate has a rival, Lady Barbara Creighton, who wears pink taffeta and has golden curls. Again, like the heroes, the marquise is moody and melancholy and often disappears.

There is a bathing scene in which two maids bathe Kate after she has been thrown from a horse. Later the marquise examines Kate's bruises.

Kate proves to be the curious heroine who gets herself into some frightening situations. Eventually, through her own resources, she solves mysteries and saves herself from the villain, the only man in the story, who wants to gain the marquise's property and will murder to do so.

The two lovers finally get together, and the formula has been completed. The heroine and the marquise see themselves as "wicked" and accept themselves as such.

Both Virga and Ramstetter seem to have tongue in cheek at times—Virga with his title of *Gaywick,* the names

Gaylord and Goodbody, and in creating all the males as homosexuals; Ramstetter, with her suggestion that the nuns, too, are lesbian, and with her character Barbara Creighton. One gets the feeling that both authors are a little shy about the genre, Virga because he scorns it slightly and Ramstetter because she seems a little hesitant about writing her story.

The Nonformula Gay Romance

Though it contains some elements of the formula, *Edward, Edward* (Macmillan), by Lolah Burford, is basically a non-category romance, telling the haunting and powerful story of a young ward, Edward, and his guardian, the Earl of Tyne, and their various levels of love for each other. The two are almost opposite: Edward, sensitive and caring; the earl, demanding and moody. The boy's identity is in question, and over the years he comes to believe he is the earl's son. He also questions his sexuality. Does he desire the earl because the older man had taken his own mother's place, or does he desire the earl because the older man denies him, thereby making himself more desirable? Is it Edward's strong yearning for the earl's company that leads Edward to homosexual activities with the earl, or is it the earl's desire, that Edward, in his love, will not refuse? Does Edward desire sexual union as well, not even admitting it fully to himself? The author does not give an easy answer. Edward is too complex a character, changing constantly in his feelings but remaining as deep within, for us to readily know him or for him to understand himself.

Tyne is a romantic type of hero. He is proud, arrogant, commanding, mysterious, sometimes cruel, sometimes kind; and he does all things—shooting, fencing, gaming—with skill. He even plays the violin brilliantly, having studied with Paganini. It is only in his sexual desires that he becomes excessive and therefore weak.

Edward goes from a child's adoration to an adult's acceptance of the earl:

It is stronger than I am, and I am never entirely going to be able to free myself, and I am never entirely going to want to.

Religious in nature, Edward almost worships the earl, who in turn acts to the boy like an unjust god: "In his will is my peace."

Various types of love and sexuality are examined here: father for son, boy for older man, man for the woman he loves, man for the courtesan. When is the attraction merely sexual? When does it become love? Can one necessarily love, or is sex enough? To Burford, love does conquer, and he who loves must suffer. The author takes us through an intricate plot with complicated characters and literally proves her point.

The sex scenes act as integral portrayals of the characters' struggles and the book's philosophy. Sadism becomes symbolic of the cruelty of life. When a character, such as Tyne, exhibits lust or sadism, the author's description takes an opposite turn from the excess of the character and becomes understated. The resultant contrast between the character's greed and violence and the author's subdued tone creates a powerful scene.

Edward's acceptance of Tyne's sadism is not so much masochism as an acceptance of love and of life itself. Burford draws a thin line between a loving and a masochistic nature, as she does between a dominating and a sadistic nature. She suggests that the dominating nature cannot be a truly loving one in that it is selfish and lacks the acceptance that is part of a deep love:

> It was not a new idea, it had been known long ago: Love suffereth long, is kind. Beareth all things, Endureth all things. Gods did not suffer, unless they became men.

Set in Regency England, the story has been well researched, so that actual personalities of the time are introduced, and the reader never questions the authenticity. The enslavement of Edward and the earl's deep concern about how he and Edward will appear to their peers are believable in a Regency context.

Setting, in this instance, helps to bring the theme to fruition. In this background, Edward develops until he painfully arrives at a stage during which he can come to terms with himself and with life. The boy is stronger than he himself is aware. Tyne sees this strength and tries to break Edward's will, since it is that will that seems to keep Edward elusive. Yet Tyne finally sees that Edward cannot be broken because there is no one thing in life that he requires. Edward can suffer defeats, but not destruction. He is resilient because he keeps a small part of himself to himself and has endless reserves. Though Tyne appears strong, always dominating, and Edward appears weak, being dominated, Edward in truth is the stronger of the two. It is he who has control, he who can choose to submit, he who can love.

These are excellent examples of characters who are in contrast, yet who complement each other. Burford uses parable-like paradox in showing the weak as strong and the strong as weak; however, rather than Christ-like, Edward is a beautiful, phoenix-like creature, burning himself out in a cruel, insensitive world, then rising from apparent consumption to renewed life and love. The last renewal that we see—for the story does not end—is Edward's choice of heterosexual love; yet we cannot believe that Tyne will leave the picture.

Limiting Your Audience

Keep in mind that any type of category writing—science fiction, Westerns, romances, and categories within these, such as Gothics and Regencies—is aimed at a particular and sometimes limited audience. To write a book solely for gays further restricts your audience. A presentation of both homosexuals and heterosexuals, such as Burford gives in *Edward, Edward,* could result in a broader readership.

XV

The Historical Romance

THE term *historical romance* has two basic meanings: (1) a romantic story leaning heavily on the past, thereby giving more meaning to the present, and (2) a story set in the past, in which the romance takes precedence over true facts. The first type of story—those by such writers as Robert Graves and Lion Feuchtwanger—is closer to a fictionalized biography, using historical happenings and characters throughout. The second type makes history suit the story.

The Cartland Stamp

The series historicals are sometimes called *Harlequins in hoopskirts*. These are sweet love stories that will fit into any setting; the time or place is unimportant. The Jacobean, Georgian, and Edwardian periods are three favorites. Since the Regency has a flavor all its own, favoring the drawing-room drama over the swashbuckling adventure, it remains in a category apart.

Barbara Cartland has been particularly successful in creating a light romantic story in which a young virgin meets a desirable, dashing hero and eventually wins him on her own terms. The Cartland heroine is intelligent and spiritual. The hero is attracted first to her beauty but eventually to her intelligence.

Cartland avoids putting men in wigs and picks her periods accordingly. At the outset, we are told the setting, which usually involves real social situations. From then on, the romance could occur in any century. Cartland is careful to describe the gowns in terms that sound delightfully glamorous for any age.

Free-lance editor Fran Fisher, who specializes in series historicals, notes that Cartland heroines differ from those in other category romances in their dialogue, education, points of view, and ideals. Cartland does relatively little description of the heroine's clothes, Fisher elaborates, characterizing her more through facial expressions, mannerisms, and dialogue. This stress on actions and comments, rather than on wardrobe, rapidly brings the heroine to life for the reader.

Through her travels—many of these tales take place in foreign lands—and her reading, the heroine has made herself an expert in some area of interest such as politics. She is able to talk intelligently to the hero. She also, if necessary, is able to help him through her area of expertise.

The Cartland heroine often is seen through the hero's eyes; *he* is reacting to *her*. Her beauty first attracts him, but her knowledge awakens his intellectual curiosity. Inspired by her, he often goes on to new achievements.

The Cartland heroine is more fully developed than is the hero. She has an idealistic and a spiritual side. She carries as her ideal the perfect love that existed between her noble parents, and she discusses with the hero the importance of a perfect love. When in trouble, she enters a chapel to pray. By suggesting that the two lovers probably knew each other in a former life, Cartland gives motivation for their present love and makes it appear eternal. A Cartland glow pervades her stories. They are pure. They are sweet. The series romances have fallen off in popularity with the advent of the sexier contemporaries. Nevertheless, they keep a loyal following.

The Bodice-Ripper

To the commercial audience, the term *historical romance* has come to mean almost exclusively the sexy historical or "bodice-ripper." These are the formula romances popular in mass-market paperback and indebted to *Gone With the Wind*. They are much longer than average romances, running to about six hundred pages. This length dictates some changes in the writer's approach. The heroine can be even more fiery and spunky than she is in the shorter romances, for she has many more opportunities to exhibit her character. Throughout trials that would leave the rest of us floundering, she is never dragged down.

Though the heroine may sometimes feel low, the reader must never feel bad with her. A depressed mood will be done in flashback or in a scene looking to a hopeful future. Romances are fantasies, and the reader is made to feel only positive emotions.

In *Gone With the Wind,* Scarlett always plans to think about things tomorrow. She doesn't dwell on what she can't handle at the moment. She knows that given enough time, she will come up with an idea. An example of her ingenuity occurs in the scene in which she uses the drapes of Tara to fashion a dress so that she can look prosperous when she visits Rhett Butler. She thinks "success" and has pride in her scheming.

All romantic heroines have a good deal of pride, not a false pride but one based on inner strength and a pride in family. Much of Scarlett's courage comes from Tara, from the land. Marilyn Granbeck's heroine in *Maura* says, "I am a Sullivan. . . . I have the Sullivan strength and determination. I will not be beaten!"

If a man does help the heroine—and of course he does from time to time—she does not feel helpless. She knows she could work something out. And the reader is told this. It is the heroine's story from beginning to end. She might save the hero, as Alaina twice saves Cole Latimer in *Ashes in the Wind*. Though it is not pointed out by the author and never expressed on tip sheets, *the heroine's feelings for the hero often control her.*

The hero, as in other romances, will parallel the heroine in strength and courage and dash. The two will therefore come together fighting, each wanting to have the upper hand. Actually, they do not at first make the perfect pair. In *Gone With the Wind,* the conflict is never resolved; but Scarlett needs Rhett, since only he can dominate her. Romance novels suggest what we do not usually see in life—that similar personalities attract, that strong needs strong and stronger. Shakespeare's *The Taming of the Shrew* gives us two such characters.

In the historical romance there is also room to develop supporting characters who both parallel and contrast with the main characters. Just as Scarlett and Rhett parallel each other in strength, so Melanie and Ashley are alike in being sweet and passive. These character traits put them in contrast with the main character and cause them to seek in Scarlett the strength, enthusiasm, and excitement they require. Though Scarlett is selfish with Melanie, the latter's acceptance of Scarlett is not based purely upon good will. It derives from the need Melanie has for such a character in her life. Similarly, Ashley's attraction to Scarlett does not derive from his sexual desire so much as from the same need for strength and hope. And Scarlett wants Ashley. To her, he stands for the Old South, the land; while to him she is the courage and hope that will make the land survive. It is Rhett, however, the one who dares to attempt to tame Scarlett, who whets the reader's fancy.

Point of View in the Historical Romance

Since the historical romance is long, you may use several points of view, showing the action from more than one vantage point. When you do change viewpoints, your transitions must be smooth so that the reader is barely aware of the switch; and a good reason must exist for your change of focus. (See Chapter 7, "Meaningful Dialogue.") However, always write the sex scenes from the heroine's viewpoint. Remember, you are telling her story and plumbing her emotions.

The Influence of Gone With the Wind

The historical-romance formula is very indebted to *Gone With the Wind*. Let's look at two novels and see which key elements of Margaret Mitchell's story they include, while incorporating their own variations. In both Granbeck's *Maura* and Woodiwiss's *Ashes in the Wind*, we start with spunky heroines, Maura and Alaina, respectively. Each girl is escaping, Maura from marriage to Braxton, a man she abhors, and Alaina, who is wanted as a spy, from both Yankees and Confederates. Neither girl immediately recognizes the hero as the right man for her, though she is physically attracted to him.

Granbeck uses the period of the first American steamboats and union strikes as a backdrop to her tale, and Woodiwiss uses the American Civil War. Though these problems influence the heroine's actions and threaten her welfare, she is in control of the story.

Such heroines need men who can dominate them: Duggan Quinn in *Maura* and Cole Latimer in *Ashes in the Wind*. These are men who do exciting things—one builds steamboats and helps to start a union, the second is an army surgeon; and both are tied into the historical background, Duggan with the union strikes and riverboat trade and Cole with the Civil War. The romance hero is more a part of the historical background than is the heroine, and that background helps to characterize him.

Historical-romance heroes are more decisive than are other men. Their decisions are made quickly, and they immediately act upon them, right or wrong. They are not men who look back and analyze. They move forward, commanding their destiny. The heroine at first resents this control and is sometimes humiliated by it. Later, she succumbs to it.

Each heroine is raped: Scarlett, by Rhett when she refuses to admit him to her bedroom; Alaina, by Cole when he is drunk. Maura is not raped by the hero but by Beau, whom she loves for a time, mistaking his character. Rape threats abound in both *Ashes in the Wind* and *Maura.* In *Gone With the Wind,* the possibility of rape is a real one for Scarlett in the South after the Civil War. In many romances, rapes are not well motivated and are included to fill the requirements of the tip sheets, not the stories.

Remember to keep rapes sensuous rather than explicit. Even committed by the villain, they should not outrage the reader. They are not presented as the acts of violence they actually are. Instead, they help to indicate that the heroine is a woman all men passionately desire.

In contrast to the hero, the other men of the story are weak, if not actually bad. *Maura* contains the evil Braxton as well as Beau, the con artist, who at first appeals to Maura. *Ashes in the Wind* shows Jacques DeBonné as the villain with no redeeming traits. *Gone With the Wind* has Ashley, who is virtuous but weak. In the historical romance, there must be a man other than the hero who figures prominently in the story.

Because of the story's length, you may bring in even more men who desire the heroine. In *Maura,* Granbeck gives us parallel characters in Braxton and Cromwell, both lusting for Maura. Cromwell also parallels Beau as a riverboat gambler. Beau, too, desires Maura rather than loving her. The one man who truly loves in these romances is the hero. Men might be shown to be infatuated with the heroine, proving her desirability, but these are in the background only. Many of the Southern young men are smitten with Scarlett, but they are insignificant in themselves.

The heroine, though strong, must be in hiding for part of the novel, thereby creating suspense. Maura is hiding from Braxton and her stepfather and searching for her brother. Alaina is hiding from the Yankees, the Confederates, and Jacques DeBonné. Scarlett must fear Yankee soldiers as she makes her way back to Tara and when she again resides there.

Each story has at least one fire from which the heroine escapes. The heroine's emotional strength at meeting almost certain death characterizes her. And she has the courage during dangerous scenes to kill, if necessary, to save herself or the man she loves. For example, Scarlett shoots a soldier who has come to Tara to pillage, and she and Melanie dispose of the body. Maura dives from a burning riverboat; and Alaina enters into a number of dangerous exploits.

History in the Romance

Though you must do your research with accuracy in mind, the historical romance often supplements fiction with only a modicum of history, and the history must suit the novel, even if facts are altered. Many historical-romance novelists start each chapter with a page or two of historical facts, thereby setting the scene and keeping the reader up to date. Actually, the more the material can be woven into the chapter as a whole, the more strength the story will possess. You will find that the true facts add a richness of detail that makes events fascinating and credible.

Rosemary Rogers in *Wicked Loving Lies* (Avon) nicely integrates history into her story by bringing in actual characters of the early nineteenth century, including Napoleon Bonaparte and Josephine. As with historical romances in general, Rogers is concerned about the historical events only as a backdrop to her tale as she takes her heroine, Marisa, from a convent school in Spain to a pirate ship, to the salons of France, and to England's social soirées. In each instance, believable characters of the time appear, playing minor roles in the story.

Suspense in the Historical Romance

The historical-romance formula gives women the chance to imagine themselves rescued by a handsome, virile hero. They can also imagine rescuing and nursing him, and eventually finding true love and happiness with him. Scenes, then, in which *he* needs *her* will occur. Duggan needs Maura's help in building the new steamship. Cole is saved and nursed by Alaina in wartime.

Two types of suspense are basic to all romances. First, apparently irreconcilable misunderstandings take place between the hero and heroine. These can last for at least half a book or more. The disagreements that are paramount are those that make us think the two never can get together. In the model, Scarlett and Rhett never really do work things out.

Second, sexual suspense predominates, especially in the bodice-ripper historicals. The repeated suggestion is made that the heroine will be undressed by the hero or by some other man. Apart from the rape and near-rape scenes, constant sexual titillation is provided. The hero and villains alike are fascinated with bare bosoms. Even if men's lives are in immediate danger, their sexual interest is not abated. The heroine, at the most unlikely moments, can be seen holding together the bodice of her gown that has recently been ripped open by some "admirer." Amid flames, pursuit, and battle, she clutches at the torn, weakened material in an attempt to preserve some last shred of dignity.

Whatever perils the hero and heroine encounter, they are aware first of a sexual desire for each other. Cole and

Alaina are trapped in a cave by their mortal enemies; he is recovering from a blow on the head, and both will soon meet death. As Alaina nurses their baby, Cole watches and forgets about their plight as he contemplates her bare bosom.

Historical romances fill the need of the woman who wants to be mobile; to live on the edge of danger and excitement, rather than boredom; to be admired and desired by many men; to be rescued and to rescue; and to make love passionately. These romances are sexual fantasies on a panoramic scale. As the saying goes, they are bigger than life.

XVI

Romantic Soaps and Sagas

Romantic Soaps

RADIO and television have accustomed us to soap operas, or soaps, so called because the sponsors were often soap companies. Such stories have entered the book world as a type of romance, also known as soaps.

Soaps tend to move more slowly than do other romances. The reactions of characters to a situation are vital. When an important event takes place, each character is told about it in turn, and we view her or his response as if a camera were focused upon the person. We hear about the occurrence over and over. What we care about is each individual's reaction to it. The writer captures the reader by involving her in the characters' problems.

Because in the soap we are examining relationships, most scenes have flashbacks, explaining who someone is or what has happened since that character has last been seen. If you were taught in writing class that flashback is a weak device, forget that rule for soaps.

Family Stories

In soaps, families are important, with characters putting the family first, right or wrong. As the family is defended, there is lots of slow, soapy conversation, often about a character's philosophy or even about death. The characters tend to be introspective, and we go into various minds rather than maintaining the single point of view. Remember, change of viewpoint calls for graceful transitions from character to character, spending some time in each.

As we get to know the characters, we learn so much about them that they seem real, and we can't help being interested in them and their problems. If they are bad, how bad can they be? If they are good, will they be victimized? Your key to a good soap will be your characterization through revelation and development. (See Chapter 4, "Character Portrayal.") You will analyze for the reader the traits of these characters, repeating your conclusions at various stages of the story. Repetition keeps the viewpoints clear for the reader.

Dwelling on dialogue, the soaps do not focus on physical descriptions, setting, the weather, or food. These are introspective dramas, and we are mainly in the mind, not on the lonely moors of the Gothics or on the travel tours of the traditional romances. You may use very little dialogue at the start of your story as you prepare the reader with character sketches. Later you will make up for this omission.

Usually a "tent-pole" character other than the protagonist holds the various elements of the story together. Everyone revolves around this figure, and her or his decisions strongly affect the lives of the others. This can be the matriarchal figure of Helen Van Slyke's *Sisters and Strangers* (Popular Library) or the father figure of *The Rich and the*

Righteous (Popular Library). In the TV series *Dallas,* Jock Ewing was the tent-pole character. When the actor who played the role died, the TV character could not be omitted from future episodes until the writers could gradually switch the viewers' focus to a new tent-pole character, Jock's wife, Miss Ellie.

The scenes that most interest the reader are those depicting wealth and power—scenes the reader won't be living. The problems that will most interest the reader are those of family—stepparents, remarriage, difficult children, sibling rivalries, mental cruelty, in-laws, abuse of some sort—any kind of domestic tragedy. The Greek tragedies showed the decline of a nobleman. To see the rich and famous fall is dramatic. The side of human nature that makes us want to see the person who has everything show a flaw is played upon by the soap writer.

As in other romances, sex scenes are sensuous, not explicit. Done well, they help to reveal character.

Examining the Heroine's Emotions

In *Season of Passion* (Dell), by Danielle Steel, we see the heroine, Kate, enter a glamorous marriage to a football hero, Tom Harper. She thereby becomes disinherited by her wealthy family. Following these emotionally charged experiences and her life with a famous man, Kate enters a life of seclusion with her son Tygue after her husband has a tragic accident. Will she find love again and relate to life as she once did? This is a low-keyed book, slowly examining the emotions of Kate in various situations. She goes from fashion model to wife to recluse and mother to a famous writer who fears her identity will be discovered.

The big scenes—the accident through which her husband is turned into the equivalent of a retarded child, and the disinheritance by her parents—are *described*. It is the talk scenes and love scenes that are *acted out*.

As we spend years with Kate in the country, accompanying her as she visits her once-famous husband who now plays Tygue's games, and seeing her concerns as a mother and a writer, we get to care about her. We become concerned about whether or not Kate will appear on a talk show. She discusses this with her agent. She refuses. She accepts. She goes through mental agonies about a TV appearance, worrying about the dress she will wear, as any woman reading the story might do herself.

A writer can show the passage of time through changes—of season, of age and interests of the characters, of clothes or design styles or even of lifestyles. Kate decides to write a book; the completion of the book, as well as repeated activities, indicates that a span of time has elapsed.

The novel is packed with power, glamour, allusions to the football world, the book and talk-show world. The reader, already in sympathy with Kate the recluse, now roots for her to come out of her comfortable but stifling cocoon into a world of allurement.

As in all soaps, the endless examining and reexamining of each situation takes place. *An idea is never presented just once.* For instance, Kate does not think Tygue should have a pony. Felicia, a friend, thinks he should. Nick, a new love, enters, and agrees with Tygue. The interest in Tygue characterizes both Felicia and Nick, and the many discussions about the pony are true to life.

This rehashing is not boring for the reader if the characterization is strong so that she identifies. Soaps are books for readers who want to slowly examine each facet of a problem. Just as we never tire of talking about ourselves and our own problems, once we have identified with these soap characters, we're quite willing to carry on our discussions in a more glamorous role.

The romance question that creates suspense in *Season of Passion* and in other soaps is, Who is Mr. Right? Sometimes the question is, Which one is he? as in Helen Van Slyke's *The Mixed Blessing* (Popular Library), which has two possible candidates.

A Man in the Major Role

Though soaps tend to be women's stories, men can play major roles, as does Joe Haylow in Van Slyke's *The Rich and the Righteous*. Joe, the powerful tent-pole character, is chairman of the giant company he himself built. The story opens at the retirement dinner at which Haylow will announce his successor. Several people are contenders for the position. Who will take Joe Haylow's place? is the question around which the entire novel revolves.

We are told in detail about each of the characters and what their chances might be. Then we flash back a year and watch the actions of these characters as they vie for power. We see them, accompanied by their spouses, interacting in the same social situations, and we view each character from a variety of perspectives.

Dialogue is often in the form of long speeches. More often, we enter the mind of each character, learning what he or she thinks of the other characters and events and what he must do to become chairman.

> Frowning, Deland methodically reviewed everything he knew about Cabot. A confirmed yes-man, an ineffectual figurehead whom Joe has accepted at the insistence of the bankers and tolerated for the sake of the stockholders. Brad was sure that Joe Haylow would welcome any excuse to replace him, but Cabot's pedestrian personality precluded any chance to legitimately remove him.

We also examine the characters' secret lives. Cabot, the company president, is having a homosexual affair. Brad Deland is having an affair with Marjorie Haylow, the wife of Haylow's minister son. Brad and his wife Doe-Doe pretend to have an acceptable marriage, so Brad can keep his position with the firm.

Most of the characters are jockeying for some position in their private lives as well as for the company chairmanship: Roger Haylow wants his father's love and approval; Joe

Haylow wants his son Woodward eventually to take the Reverend Jimmy Jackson's place as leading minister; Cabot wants sex thrills and the chairmanship; Deland wants power above love.

In soaps, we see the power plays of the wealthy, the famous, the beautiful. Not many scenes show action. Mostly, characters talk over what has happened or what might happen. The action tends to be described in paragraphs interspersed with dialogue. Soaps are not intricate stories. The premise can be set down in a sentence or two.

The Rich and the Righteous is not concerned with setting, weather, or food. Since the business involved is a fashion corporation, clothes are mentioned, but how they look is relatively unimportant. We are watching, instead, a proud family that could fall apart. On the surface it looks good— one son is a minister with a "happy" marriage; the other is an executive in the family business. Beneath these facades, troubles fester. We are also watching business associates, another kind of family, all bright and able to handle the chairmanship; yet underneath the surface, how far will each character go to win the prize? The parallel structure adds importance to private and business conflicts. Forewarnings in soaps hint at future unethical conduct and create suspense.

Romantic Sagas

History was once passed on by word of mouth. The Icelandic people were noted for their long narratives about the exploits of heroes of heroic families. These sagas, as they were called, were committed to memory and learned by each generation in turn. The term eventually came to apply to stories about any heroic achievement or grand adventure.

The romantic saga is not about true heroes or heroines, though the characters are strong and decisive. The tales are about exciting events that would not happen to the average reader. Often they are generation novels, following the activities of an entire family and showing the family's rise and fall. This family, ideally, is rich and powerful or becomes rich and powerful. The lead character should change the lives of those around him.

The Family or Generation Saga

Janet Dailey has added to romantic saga literature with *This Calder Sky* (Pocket), set in Montana. It tells the tale of the interactions of the O'Rourke and Calder families, in particular Maggie O'Rourke and Chase Calder. Dailey, a popular Harlequin and Silhouette writer, has extended the tale of a typical Harlequin heroine, Maggie, who at fifteen first learns about sex from Chase Calder. The Calder ranch is huge, and the small ranchers cannot hope to compete with the "king" of this ranching empire, Webb Calder. Maggie's father, Angus O'Rourke, decides that since Chase has had his daughter, Angus will steal Calder cattle. This action leads to his own death at Webb Calder's hands.

As in all romances, when the heroine is in need, the opportunity she has hoped for presents itself. In this case, Maggie's aunt in California agrees to have Maggie stay with her, and she does not object when she learns Maggie is pregnant. Through her aunt, Maggie meets Dr. Phillip Gordon, who is much older. Maggie loves his tenderness and his interest in her son, Ty. Eventually they marry, and through him Maggie's cultural education is completed.

When Phillip conveniently dies (offstage) of a heart attack, Ty runs off to find his natural father. Maggie, now a polished, elegant lady, follows her son to Montana. There she clashes with Chase Calder, whom she still loves. The family structure gives Dailey a chance to build the material into several books.

The strength of the story is in the Montana segments. The decline of Culley O'Rourke, Maggie's brother, and the crumbling of the O'Rourke ranch stand in sharp contrast to Maggie's rise. Her brother's hatred contrasts with Maggie's forgiving, loving nature. Buck, like a brother to Chase, parallels Culley's decline, as the two fall, through greed and hatred. The father-son team of Culley and Angus are contrasted with the Calder father and son.

Maggie and Chase parallel one another in that they are strong and determined, yet loving. Their son, Ty, apparently will take after them, and the Calder empire will continue.

Unusual plot twists add suspense. Webb Calder's coming after Angus O'Rourke, the threats to Chase Calder, and Buck's surprising role add power to the tale.

The Classic Saga

A classic generation saga is John Galsworthy's *The Forsyte Saga* (Scribner's), which follows the fortunes of a powerful nineteenth- and twentieth-century English family whose members put material goods above other interests. Such an attitude characterizes the Victorian man of property, unconcerned about the social evils of his day. Weak links in the family structure are those members who care for the arts, and those who are able to care deeply for other human beings.

For family sagas, the nineteenth and twentieth centuries are still preferred, as are Northern European families. Characters struggling for freedom of expression against a tight family and social order are lifelike and intriguing.

Whether you choose to depict the exploits of a single heroine or of an entire family, the romantic soaps and sagas allow you to include a male viewpoint, to depict real activities in actual settings as a backdrop to the heroine, and to fully develop your characters. Well written, these genres do very well on the commercial market.

XVII

The Contemporary Romance

Love and Sex

Many readers have moved out of the home and into offices, and are no longer content with tales of innocent young heroines unable to support themselves. The new heroines are older, from twenty-six to forty-five, depending upon the line. And they are more self-sufficient than were earlier heroines.

The new heroine has gained success in the working world, so her needs have changed. In contemporary romances, the heroine works side by side with the hero. If she intends to stop work, we are assured that she will in some way continue to be fulfilled in the future by expressing her talents. In Kingston's *Winter Love Song* the heroine and hero, both ski champions, will jointly operate a ski resort.

Motherhood is desirable and planned for, but the contemporary heroine will not give up her position; she will take time off. In the contemporary romance the heroine will be fulfilled in every aspect of her life: sex, home, work, leisure. This heroine, however, gets what she wants not by remaining pure but by sleeping with the man she desires. Sex is the honey that draws the bee; and she is generous in doling out the honey, usually with protestations that she cannot help herself.

The Superstructure

The length of the contemporary romance will allow you to develop strong subplots to reinforce the main story. The setting is important, giving us a fresh look into an ordinary place or taking us to new territory. We might also take a look at a little-known occupation.

Willa Lambert, in *Love's Emerald Flame* (Harlequin Superromance), at the outset gets her leading characters together with a cute meet. Diana Green, a journalist who is in Peru to do research for a travel article, is eating at a restaurant when a handsome stranger joins her and orders a meal. He acts as if he knows her, calls her "darling," then suddenly disappears. This is a novel way to bring the hero onto the scene, and the incident starts a mystery that intertwines with the romance. Diana's life is threatened, and, as the tour continues, the mysterious stranger keeps reappearing.

In such a story, the author's main problem will be character motivation. Lambert must have a good reason for Diana to be writing a story on Machu Picchu so that the heroine will leave the tour and stay there, alone. Lambert has to make us believe that Diana is courageous enough to go into the jungle on a dangerous mission. To solve the problem, Lambert lets the reader know that Diana, at home, had done a story on drugs for which she had made illicit buys for the police. Lambert adds irony by establishing that Diana is in Peru because her mother thinks she can't get into trouble with her journalist's curiosity while traveling with a tour.

The hero's motives must also be carefully established. He is risking his life for family honor. The reader must believe that he would do so.

The Superromance gives Lambert room to bring in supporting characters such as George Culhaney, who once discovered some ruins, but was fought off by native tribesmen and could never again find the site. The author's use of George gives Diana a chance to learn more about the jungle. And we learn how easily one could be lost there forever. We are, then, far more anxious when Diana wants to enter its depths with Sloane, a stranger. George's inability to find the lost ruins parallels Sloane's search for the downed plane, filled with artifacts, the plane he must find to remove the stain on his family's name. Diana's roommate on the tour, Carol, who lacks the true spirit of adventure, is used to set off Diana's good judgment and spunky nature. *Love's Emerald Flame* is an example of the weaving and unweaving of misunderstandings, while the characters traverse fascinating terrain.

The Changing Love Scene

In 1978, Simon & Schuster, which once distributed Harlequins through Pocket Books, entered the field of romance, using U.S. authors and settings. Then, in 1980, Dell Candlelight Romances launched Ecstasy Candlelights, which now act as models for the contemporary formula. The Ecstasy line encourages the use of ethnic heroines and heroes.

The love scenes in contemporaries are sensuous. Eventually, sometimes more than once, the love is consummated. The Ecstasy formula calls for more sex outside of marriage, although the way the author handles her characters determines how much sex she will include. However, the marriage of convenience has been overworked.

The Divorced or Widowed Heroine

Jove's Second Chance at Love series paved the way for a new type of heroine, one who has already had her first marriage. This format gives the writer an opportunity to construct a more intricate story, since the heroine is starting again after a past love. The old love is still in the picture, but the love relationship has concluded before the start of the novel. The old love is a minor character who must not distract us from the new love.

We have seen how Meredith Kingston used the cute meet in *Winter Love Song,* as Felicia encounters her former husband, Grant, on the ski slopes. What we quickly learn is that Felicia had left Grant five years ago, not telling him she was pregnant because she knew that Grant could not settle down from the glamorous ski-resort life. When Felicia meets Grant five years later, he supposes the little girl is the child of Felicia's second husband.

A story such as this, structured around one character's missing years of information and the necessity for the other character to add lie to lie, results in any number of misunderstandings.

Kingston makes it clear that her characters are still in love. Her plot gives her a chance to bring in several plausible sex scenes with both characters trying to recapture the past, still feeling, in a sense, that they belong to each other.

The ski setting lends itself nicely to the moment of danger, as Grant rescues Felicia from the snow. Kingston makes her setting an integral part of the story, letting it add to the suspense.

Setting also plays a part in the turning point for Felicia. Grant has insisted that Felicia take the resort he had planned to develop. Her daughter looks at the glistening mountain and asks, "Does this belong to us?"

And suddenly Felicia remembered that it did. This was hers, it belonged to her, and she could make of it whatever she wanted: a defeat or a victory. And at

that moment she decided that she wasn't going to
turn away from the challenge. This time she was
going to stay in the race.

Just as the metaphor fits the ski world, so does Kingston's
use of irony. As Grant watches his daughter ski, he is impressed and comments, "It's a shame her father couldn't
have seen her today. He would have really had something
to brag about."

Ilse, the "other woman," threatens at each turn to take
Grant back to Europe and away from Felicia just as the
latter becomes more aware that she still loves him. We
also see that Ilse had played a role in the first breakup.
However, our strong hero and heroine are able to override
such a character. The protagonists of a romance should finally resolve their own problems. An outside character
should never be introduced to help them solve their
differences.

Problems with the Category

The formulas of some of the contemporary romances are
difficult to work with while achieving good taste and
doing satisfactory writing. To keep the couple at odds, sex
scenes are sometimes interrupted. Starting a couple on a
passionate course and breaking them off just prior to the
final union will not ring true in most instances. Motivat-
ing several such scenes in one book will call for great skill.
In this type of plotting, sex scenes rarely seem integral
parts of the story. Instead, they may appear as a series of
superimposed, titillating moments.

Authors are warned in the tip sheets that the heroine
must love the hero before she has sex with him. In this
case, sex and love are synonymous. The directive actually
means that you should tell the reader that the heroine is
physically attracted to the hero, that this is someone she
could care about, or that she cares about him and doesn't
yet know it. But is that love? Passionate as the kisses are,

the author cannot make the reader believe in love if the couple gets together too early in the story and too easily. Sex and love are not separable in a contemporary romance formula.

Modern Themes

Specialized Minorities

Some authors are taking advantage of a widely read genre to present issues dealing with specialized minorities while still keeping within the aura of romance. In *The Rainbow Chase* (Gallen/Pocket), as by Kris Karron, Carol Norris depicts a hero whose wife has died because she would not have a mastectomy.

Norris has written two romances for the deaf reader, a minority that has been almost totally ignored throughout the history of book publishing. Rachel Ryan in *Eloquent Silence* (Dell Candlelight Ecstasy) and Celeste de Blasis in *The Tiger's Woman* (Delacorte) also handle deaf characters. Norris's Gothic *Island of Silence* (by Caroline Brimley Norris, Popular Library, reprinted by Alinda Press) is assigned reading in twelve colleges and universities. The story depicts a hero, deafened in Vietnam. Emotionally shattered, he refuses to accept the help of the heroine, who has been hired to teach him to communicate. She can sign because her little sister, a rubella baby, was born deaf. At first the heroine must protect herself from the deaf hero by allowing him to believe the conclusion he has jumped to—that she is deaf:

> I spelled to show him I could communicate soundlessly with him. But he was as ignorant as the rest. His lips parted, eyes narrowed under the dark, arching brows.
> "*You* are deaf, *too*! You're a *deaf* girl!" He released me.

Let the mistake stand, for his sake and my safety. I nodded, and signed, "I am deaf." Point to my ear (both ears for clarity), then hands together: "closed." "Ears closed." Deaf. Nodding. Lying.

"But you can understand what I say?" He marveled. "How can you understand?"

I put my fingertips delicately on his lips, signed "see" with V-fingers from my eyes to his lips.

"You lip-read? You lip-read that well? I try and try, but I can't lip-read a single sentence!"

No deaf girl could have lip-read in that light. At best, an expert speech-reader can catch one quarter of the words and guess the rest. Anything more was myth, and he believed the myth, like most hearing people, and was frozen in awe and hope.

I backed away to a safe distance, my arms aching, backed toward the door.

"Who are you? Why do you look like her? I mean, did Ken . . . plan *that,* too? How could he? You're *deaf* . . . ! Oh, my God."

A handicap can add to the drama of the characters' lines, making a romance even more intense.

Celeste De Blasis's novel *The Night Child* is a Gothic tale. The child, Missy, whom the governess, Brandy, comes to help, is a secondary autistic child. This is a child who seems to have developed normally but, through some terrible shock, reacts like a child with infantile autism. Such a child, according to De Blasis, "has repetitive behavior with the hands, seems to see right through another person, ceases to speak, ceases to function normally whatsoever." It has been found, the author asserts, that a child must be extremely intelligent to exert enough self-discipline to shut out the world.

Missy's father is under the impression that she blames him for her mother's death in a barn fire. The governess who comes begins to believe that perhaps he was responsible. We learn that Missy has been warned by the actual murderer that if she tells anyone what she knows, the father, too, will die. Missy, in an enormous act of will, has done her best to protect the one person left in the world whom she loves.

This romance, too, is taught in colleges and universities. Despite tip sheets which do not admit to themes other than love, writers are including meaningful material that is attracting romance readers.

The Ethnic Romance

In June 1980, Dell Publishing Company released the first category romance featuring a black heroine. Since that time, a variety of ethnic novels has appeared, with Indian, Hispanic, black, and Oriental protagonists.

The ethnic romances are concerned with the life situations that face a particular group, as well as with the classic love story. For instance, Jean Hager's *Portrait of Love* (Dell Candlelight) depicts the love of a teacher heroine and a painter hero, both Cherokee Indians in Northeastern Oklahoma, where the Cherokee nation was established. Besides the Cherokee setting, Hager includes some Cherokee mythology.

Marisa de Zavala, author of *Golden Fire, Silver Ice* (Dell Candlelight Ecstasy), says, "You worry yourself to death thinking, 'Am I meeting the formula the way the editors want it?' " As a Mexican-American, she found the tip sheets didn't apply to her culture. How could she talk about Mexican-Americans "without at least mentioning the existence of a political organization"? Then she worried that editors didn't want religion included. "I don't know how you can talk about a Mexican-American without talking about the Catholic Church." Furthermore, she had read tip sheets that said not to bring in the family. She wondered how she could create a Mexican-American character without a family. "So I went ahead and did all these things. . . . It's been very exciting for me to be able to write about Mexican-Americans who are inner-directed people, who are intelligent and attractive. I like dispelling the stereotype."

As an ethnic writer, you may not only face the unique situation of having to depart from the tip sheets to be true to the group you are depicting, but also you may want to combine more than one minority issue, as does Lia Sanders in *The Tender Mending* (Dell Candlelight Ecstasy). In this black romance between a heroine photographer and a hero doctor, the author gives substance to the basic misunderstandings by including a real social problem for any race: child abuse.

In trying new themes, ask yourself two questions: (1) Does the idea I present add drama? and (2) Does the tone of my entire work remain romantic? If you can answer "yes" to both questions, you may want to submit a romance on a fresh topic.

XVIII

The Young Adult Romance

The Formula

YOUNG adult romances caught on like *Wildfire*, the name of one of the early Scholastic lines. The formula is geared to the young person eleven or twelve or older, with a fifteen- or sixteen-year-old heroine, since young people prefer a heroine older than they are. The hero is a year or two years older than the heroine. As in adult romances, the story is told from the heroine's viewpoint. She is confronted with problems and uncertainties, especially about her first romantic encounters. Through facing these situations with spirit, she grows. Again, her ambivalence is an important ingredient, and misunderstandings create much of the suspense.

Your young adult heroine is a teenage, Harlequin Romance type of girl, placed in an American high school. Your settings can include typical teenage meeting places, though spots where young people go with their families, such as beach or ski resorts, add variety. Popular settings include movie theaters, swimming parties, summer camp, or school dances. The settings are middle-class, suburban backdrops that don't include prostitution or the use of drugs. Most of the readers are located in small towns or cities and that is what they want to read about. The atmosphere is wholesome.

The problems for your heroine are those facing any high school girl:

1. Who is she, and why does she feel different from the crowd? She might fantasize about being one of the more popular girls in the group, since most teenagers will identify more easily with a heroine who is a little shy, especially about sex.

2. How should she act on a first date?

3. Should she go steady? What if her parents object?

4. Do her parents disapprove of her boyfriend? Her crowd?

5. What should she do if she and her best friend like the same boy?

6. How should she relate to divorced parents?

7. How can she manage to meet the new boy in town?

8. How can she compete with the class flirt?

9. What if the boy gets too serious? What if he wants to get married?

10. How should she react, having lost the lead in the school play or not made the basketball team, etc.? The problems are endless and very real, as she attempts to work through difficult life situations for the first time.

The hero is a nice guy, but the heroine will probably pick another, Mr. Charm himself, before she grows enough to look for qualities in character. She is innocent and spunky, working out her own dilemmas rather than depending upon the adults in the story, though they may give her valuable advice. She grows in the story through learning more about herself and about life. Romance is a part of her life, not her entire focus. The plots for young adults can therefore be stronger than those for most adult lines, incorporating subplots, growth of character, and theme.

Before attempting to write young adult stories of any type, the writer must know the language, the trends, and the deep concerns of the teenager. This is an age group to write for only if you know it well. Remembrances of your own youth may not be vivid enough or may not help you to successfully depict today's young person. Though the books are shorter than adult romances, they are not easier to write, unless you truly know that world. It is possible to learn about it (see Chapter 20, "Accurate Research").

Two Classics

A writer can take one of two approaches in writing about young adults. Either she looks at the world of the young from the viewpoint of an adult and, through entering the young person's mind, puts the whole in adult perspective, or she sees the whole from the young person's standpoint. Young adult romances have the latter perspective. In order to understand both points of view, you would do well to study a classic of each type.

The Death of the Heart

Elizabeth Bowen's *The Death of the Heart* (Vintage) sensitively portrays for adults an innocent sixteen-year-old girl, Portia Quayne, as she reaches out, demanding love that no one is prepared to offer her. Portia is the half-sister of Tom Quayne, an advertising man. Not really wanted, she lives with Tom and his wife, Anna, after Portia's mother dies.

Portia falls in love with Eddie, who works for Quayne. She becomes disillusioned with Eddie when he proves his selfishness and his lack of real interest in her. To climax this humiliation, she discovers that Anna has been reading her diary.

Portia then runs away to Major Brutt, a retired army officer and family friend, pleading with him to marry her. The idea is preposterous; however, Portia sees that his situation parallels her own in that both are tolerated, not really belonging. The major alerts the others, and they have a family conference to decide how to get her back. They finally send the housekeeper, the one who has always taken Portia for granted, thus making the girl feel she belongs.

The opening of the story prepares us for the brittleness to come:

> That morning's ice, no more than a brittle film, had cracked and was now floating in segments. These tapped together or, parting, left channels of dark water, down which swans in slow indignation swam.

Portia, like the swans, will go her solitary and indignant way, never understanding that those around her cannot give as much as she expects of them. They are as baffled by her demands for love as she is by their refusal.

Flambards

K. M. Peyton's *Flambards* (World) is a story seen through Christina Parson's eyes. We are not adults, relating to the situation. We are living with her the life of a twelve-year-old orphan of the Edwardian period, growing up at Flambards with her Uncle Russell and cousins Mark and Will. Christina learns to love the decaying Victorian mansion, Flambards, and to love horses, as do her uncle and Mark. She hates the class system, however, as she sees these two tyrannize the servants, thoughtless of both man and beast. Will hates horses and spends his time on airplane models and designs. Horses and planes become symbols of the two ways of life: the old, decaying life of the landed gentry and the new, mechanized life of the future and World War I. Christina is caught between two worlds. She is the transition figure. As Will clashes with his father and Mark, she is trapped between the passions of the disparate viewpoints.

For the young, the pull of the new and of love is stronger. Book 2, *The Edge of the Cloud,* is the moving love story of Will and Christina. "We've eloped," Christina exclaims to her aunt Grace when with Will, Christina arrives at Battersea, not yet married, and without money or luggage in a borrowed Rolls-Royce.

Aunt Grace insists that before they marry, Will must get a job and money. While he works on planes as a mechanic and test pilot, Christina obtains a job in a nearby hotel. Though Christina gives up a good deal to stand by Will, especially since she is terrified of flying, we never feel she has sacrificed herself. She is strong, she is sharing life with someone she loves. True, she is helping him to fulfill his dream, but it is the dream of an idealist, the dream of a century, the vision from which the future will be formed. Christina sharing Will's vision is Christina bravely living toward the future, Christina defying her uncle and his wish that she marry Mark, Christina refusing to stay tied to old traditions.

The Theme of Love

Coming to terms with love is a recurrent premise in romances dealing with young adults. Melinda Pollowitz's *Princess Amy* (Bantam Sweet Dreams) is a good example of a sensitive young adult romance with this theme. Amy is a sixteen-year-old girl being forced to spend a month on Mackinac Island with rich relatives she doesn't like. She is an individual, and she feels she does not fit into this fast crowd. She cultivates the friendship of two young people who are not acceptable to the group because they are not afraid to be different: Amber and Peter.

Attempting to be herself, Amy does feel lonely at times, especially when she will not enter into an ongoing game of Dungeons and Dragons, finding it ridiculous. The game gets the crowd into trouble and puts Amy in dangerous situations. Amy is very attracted to Guy, the leader of the Dungeons and Dragons game and of the wealthy social set of young people, but she finally chooses the not-so-popular Pete.

Sex scenes in young adult romances consist of a touch or a light kiss only. Mostly they stress the heroine's reactions to touches and kisses. Since these are her first experiences, there is a heightened emotion, creating a dramatic effect.

> "You really are a different sort then, aren't you, fair lady?" Guy reached out and touched her cheek gently with one finger. "I like that. I surely do. . . . Now quit looking out from under your eyelashes at me like that. It's very sexy, you know."

Amy's reaction to the scene:

> *He makes me feel so beautiful. Even if he did nearly drown me. Nobody ever called me things like princess and lady fair before. I didn't even know I did that looking-out-from-under-my-eyelashes trick. Wonder if it's as good as flirting?*

One of Amy's problems, a big one to her, is that she doesn't know how to flirt. Another is that she likes to eat, whereas her aunt and all the other girls are on perpetual diets to be super-thin. Her aunt would rather she conform and be popular than be different. And she is concerned about clothes. But her real problem is, what is romantic love?

> Amy relaxed back against Guy's chest and they sailed the boat all the way back to the Painter's dock. She felt warm and almost safe in Guy's arms. A shooting star streaked down the black sky, and with fingers crossed she watched it arc out of sight. *Wish I may, wish I might. Is this what love feels like? Like this, right now. Tonight?*

Gradually she learns that love is more comfortable than

shooting stars. Love is the concern that Pete has for her; it is not Guy's putting her on a pedestal and calling her princess. Love is taking responsibility and being there when you're needed, as Pete is when he rescues her from her fall from a horse. And love is appreciating the other's concern and responsibility. Love likes you as you are, not as you might be if you dieted down two sizes or played the proper part of princess in a game to alleviate boredom. Amy learns and grows, but we feel the seeds for that growth were planted long ago and tended carefully, so that one month just adds a small spurt of growth to the already green and thriving sprout.

Lucille S. Warner takes a different approach to the young adult romance formula in *Love Comes to Anne* (Scholastic Wildfire). The suspense here is not a question of which young man the heroine will choose but of what she will do, actually having fallen in love. True love at sixteen is far from easy.

Anne, a popular girl, meets and falls in love with Pierre, an exchange student from France, who is older. He is repeating a year of school in order to improve his English. The author takes us from the problem, Why doesn't he call? to, Should I go back to France with him and marry him? The dilemma is a moving one for the reader, who feels Anne and Pierre are truly right for each other. Will either ever meet another one so right? But should Anne give up her senior year of high school? Should she give up college? Her opportunities will be cut short by an early marriage.

Anne grows as she loves Pierre. She learns that love makes her feel complete; but she also learns that love is difficult and calls for moments of real trial. She sees the frightening side of making a lasting commitment. Pierre knows what he wants in life—to run the family winery—but is Anne ready to settle down to married life without knowing what her other options are?

Young adult formulas usually insist on a happy ending, and we have a semisweet one here. Anne has many exciting things ahead of her. Pierre will wait and hope.

. . . maybe it would be Pierre one day far ahead.
Maybe it would be to someone as yet undreamed of.
But whenever the moment came, and through all the
time until it came, nothing would ever be quite the
same as this had been, nothing would ever again be
quite so magical.

Helping a young girl come gently out of her fantasy and
face reality can be a real contribution by a writer to the
young audience.

The teenage romance is 40,000 to 50,000 words as opposed to the adult 55,000 to 90,000 words or longer.
More minor characters can be introduced than in the adult
romances because the teenage girl is certainly going to
have a family and friends rather than being the homeless
waif of many adult stories. Romance is a part of her life,
not her entire focus. The plots for young adults can therefore be stronger, incorporating subplots, parallelism,
growth of character, and theme.

Breaking the Formula

Barbara Conklin set out to write a gripping romance about
young love in *P. S. I Love You*. Unaware that she should
have a happy ending, she wrote a tragic one and suc-
ceeded. As we've seen, it is sometimes possible to break
out of the formula and still sell within the category.

In Conklin's story, Mariah, sixteen, wants to be a romance writer and has stashed away in her closet tales by
Rosemary Rogers, Kathleen E. Woodiwiss, and Susan
Howatch. She is in the fantasy stage of life, dreaming
about her first kiss. Her mother takes a summer house-sit-
ting job in Palm Springs, forcing Mariah and her kid sister, Kim, to leave Laguna Beach, since their house has
been rented. Mariah's parents are separated, and her father
has been in an accident and unable to send support.

At Palm Springs, Mariah meets Paul Strobe and gets
over one of her prejudices, that all rich people are snobs.

Mariah must learn to accept Paul as he is and to apologize for having been prejudiced. Her mother must learn a parallel lesson regarding her former husband.

A nice touch to the love story is that the games Mariah and Paul play with each other don't work. Each pretends to be popular, she with a boyfriend and he with a girlfriend. They only hurt and confuse one another with the lies. It is when they are most themselves that they are most appealing.

Young adult romances often have a theme. This one is stated by a minor character: "Time is so awfully short for us humans. We have no right to play God with it." Mariah learns as well that money can't buy everything. It can't save Paul. For her, the bumper sticker *P. S. I Love You,* the *P. S.* standing for Palm Springs, takes on quite a different, bittersweet meaning: Paul Strobe.

Though the ending is sad, it is satisfying. Both mother and daughter have grown, and their lives have been enriched through suffering. Mariah's parents are reconciled. Mariah's love for Paul has remained unimpaired. Time cannot now tarnish it, and that is the best possible ending for a romance.

Rooted in Reality

In the young adult romances, a meaningful relationship is stressed. A first kiss becomes the high point of action. The love develops slowly, timidly, until that kiss, after which the story ends. The stories say to the young teenage girl, "Everyone has the same doubts that you have. Nobody is perfect. Have confidence in yourself. The boy-girl relationship isn't so scary as you thought." These young heroines have high standards; and what young girls do not wistfully long for love while being terrified of the real thing? Yes, the heroine is pretty and doesn't seem to have the problems or the imagined problems that beset most girls at adolescence—crooked teeth, straight hair when curly is the fashion, curly hair when straight is in style, skin that reacts to chocolate, myopic eyes, obesity. She is surprisingly level-headed. But these are fantasy heroines. These are the dream girls readers would like to be.

In spite of the fact that young adult romances are superficially unreal, the heroine's emotional life is rooted in reality. She is not the insecure girl of the Gothics. She is attempting to gain a better idea of her identity through the relationships with those around her. The issue of identity is more prominent in the young adult romances than in the other categories and presents a healthy picture to the teenage reader.

Teenage romances have a longer "shelf life" than do adult romances, since a new audience comes along every few years. If you know young people and can express their needs, their fears, and their desires, this may be the market for you.

XIX

Overcoming Writer's Block

A writing block can result from taking yourself too seriously. You've heard stories about writers being unable to write after creating a best seller. Success frightens some; it makes others compete too energetically with themselves. A blank page, with three hundred pages left to fill, frightens both professional and would-be authors.

Visualization

Anxiety will interfere with the creative process. You must practice ways to control stress. Deep breathing, followed by mental images of yourself at work with words flowing freely, will get your mind on the right track.

If you are a beginning writer, you may lack the courage to get started. The visualization technique will help you to see yourself as a writer. Visualization is part of the creative process, and it can help to make you more creative.

Unpublished writers often feel intimidated by those who have been published. Avoid explaining that you haven't yet published. Always be a writer in your own mind; then live up to the writer's task of getting down to work.

Avoiding Procrastination

Procrastination is not writer's block. Don't use suggestions from Chapter 20, "Accurate Research," to keep yourself from work. Clipping for your file is done after or before writing hours.

Talking your story is not putting it on paper. Don't feel that because you've told your story to someone, you've done your job for the moment.

Patricia Matthews says, "I had friends who never worked outside the home and still procrastinated and couldn't get anything done. While working, I turned out more material than they did by writing just a couple of pages a night. You don't have to do a lot of pages, I found out, as long as you do them steadily. It's like saving money. You put a little bit away, a little bit away, and it amounts up. I did my Gothics that way."

Discipline

Writing is like any other job. You will keep definite hours. If a ringing phone is your nemesis, take the receiver off the hook or get an answering machine. Let people know what your working hours are. They'll forget, but keep reminding them.

LaVyrle Spencer does not believe in a tight writing schedule. "I think it's absolute nonsense. Nobody can create every single day." She had read that if you want to be a writer, you have to write every day and anywhere and everywhere, learning to shut out what's around you. "That summer I almost alienated my family permanently by taking my notebook to the ball games when they were playing. At the same time I probably looked like the most pompous person to the people around me. Well, I was doing what the books told me. Now I'm a full-time writer, but that probably means fifty percent of the time I'm creating and fifty percent of the time I'm doing business."

Betty Layman Receveur (*Molly Gallagher,* Ballantine) writes every day: "I've found that if you do not make your living at writing—and I've been on both sides of the fence—you use all kinds of excuses . . . because writing is tremendously hard. Maybe you're ill and today's just not the day. 'I'm tired, and I don't feel like it.'

"Once you start to make a living out of writing, I really think you take a different attitude about it. I don't think there's ever a time now when I say, 'I just don't have it today. I just can't do it.' I have even had the flu, and I would take a pad and pencil and lie on the couch, make notes, and do a little bit anyhow. And I've found there are days when I really don't feel like working, but I go ahead and do it. I go back later and read over the material. I can't tell any difference between the material I did when I didn't feel like working and the material I did when it was a wonderful day and I thought, 'Oh, yes, let me at the typewriter.' "

Story Blocks

Are you doing enough research on your setting, foreign or local, past or present, to spark ideas? Are you making use of the distinctive flavor of that community?

In a period piece, ask yourself what was happening of interest that could affect your characters. What interesting people were living then? When planning *The Reluctant Duke,* I wondered how the practice of Friedrich Mesmer (1733–1815), who used an early form of hypnosis to treat patients, could influence my Regency characters. I brought in Doctor Linse, a fictitious character who had studied with Mesmer in Vienna. Julia finds a way of forcing Linse to teach her how to "mesmerize." She then tries her newly acquired skill on the reluctant duke. Julia's determination to learn mesmerism is an element of subplot that finally helps the two lovers to unite.

Related Art Forms

If you can't get started or feel you have nothing at the moment to say, perhaps you aren't "priming the pump." Are you keeping the formula in mind by reading romances?

Continually refreshing your talent with other art forms will also help to guard against any writer's block.

Plays

If you are bogged down because your characters just don't come out with clever comments, try reading plays aloud or acting out plays with a friend. The sophisticated comedies of Oscar Wilde will be just the thing to get your mind working on witty banter.

> JACK: I am in love with Gwendolen. I have come up to town expressly to propose to her.
> ALGERNON: I thought you had come for pleasure. . . . I call that business.
> JACK: How utterly unromantic you are.
> ALGERNON: I really don't see anything romantic in proposing. It is very romantic to be in love. But there is nothing romantic about a definite proposal. Why, one may be accepted. One usually is, I believe. Then the excitement is all over. The very essence of romance is uncertainty. If ever I get married, I'll certainly try to forget the fact.
> JACK: I have no doubt about that, dear Algy. The

Divorce Court was specially invented for people whose memories are so curiously constituted.

ALGERNON: Oh! there is no use speculating on that subject. Divorces are made in Heaven. . . .

Complete the scene between Jack and Algernon. What is Jack's response to Algernon's pronouncement? What would Jack say to Gwendolen? How would Algernon react were he in love?

Write a scene of dialogue between two of your own characters. Show the hero feeling superior to the heroine and her verbal reactions.

If you want to write Regencies or historicals, you'll enjoy Oliver Goldsmith's *She Stoops to Conquer*. Here, Miss Hardcastle is meeting her friend:

MISS HARDCASTLE: I'm glad you're come, Neville, my dear. Tell me, Constance, how do I look this evening? Is there any thing whimsical about me? Is it one of my well-looking days, child? Am I in face today?

MISS NEVILLE: Perfectly, my dear. Yet now I look again—bless me!—sure, no accident has happened among the canary birds or the gold fishes? Has your brother or the cat been meddling? Or has the last novel been too moving?

MISS HARDCASTLE: No; no thing of all this. I have been threatened—I can scarce get it out—I have been threatened with a lover.

Using exaggeration and surprise, write a scene of dialogue between two of your own characters.

For pure romance, read Edmond Rostand's *Cyrano de Bergerac*. If you think for a minute that dialogue isn't important, remember that it is Cyrano's *words* that win the heart of Roxanne for the handsome Christian, who has no talent for words. Unfortunately, too many heroes resemble Christian in their dialogue. A character with the looks of Christian and the soul and tongue of Cyrano would charm any heroine. *Hear* what characters from plays are saying, and dialogue will flow more readily.

Poetry

Reading poetry is perhaps the best way to keep in tune with your emotions. Once certain emotions are evoked, you may remember incidents long forgotten.

In Samuel Taylor Coleridge's romantic "Kubla Khan," we are transported to the mystical kingdom of Xanadu. Let a portion of his words carry you into the exotic mood:

> A damsel with a dulcimer
> In a vision once I saw:
> It was an Abyssinian maid,
> And on her dulcimer she played,
> Singing of Mount Abora.
> Could I revive within me
> Her symphony and song,
> To such a deep delight 'twould win me
> That with music loud and long,
> I would build that dome in air,
> That sunny dome! those caves of ice!
> And all who heard should see them there,
> And all should cry, Beware! Beware!
> His flashing eyes, his floating hair!
> Weave a circle round him thrice,
> And close your eyes with holy dread,
> For he on honey-dew hath fed,
> And drunk the milk of Paradise.

Poets, with their expression of heightened emotional response, can lift us to new visions.

Art

Several hours in a museum or with books on art will enliven your creative mind and spark ideas. If you are working on a historical piece, visit some of the real characters of that period through portraits, or actually see some of the landscapes or battles. What do you learn about the American nineteenth century through Winslow Homer? What does Sir Thomas Lawrence tell you about Romantic characters? Do John Constable's Gothic spires, rainbows, and pastoral scenes truly lead your mind to the sublime as the Gothic ladies supposed?

Sometimes portraits can help get involved in characters of your own. Ask yourself questions about the painting. for instance, in John Singer Sargent's "Doctor Pozzi at Home" (1881), the doctor has a seemingly tranquil face but expressive eyes. His stance, with one hand resting on the front of his robe and the other on the cord by his hip, and one leg thrust forward, tells us something about his manner. His graceful hands, too, are clues to his identity. What questions do you have about Dr. Pozzi? What might some answers be? You may lead yourself into a fresh character or story.

Music

Music will surely help you to be in touch with your deeper feelings. Listening to music while you actually are writing can keep you from concentrating on your own rhythms. But music is valuable to relax the mind, to quiet that analytical, worrying left side of the brain so that your intuitive right side can be heard.

Symphonies on which the left side of the brain can concentrate, while the right side makes intuitive leaps to new ideas in your story, can end that block. Planning a story to music results in free-flowing ideas. You can later let the left side of the brain, that side that loves to analyze, put your ideas into step-by-step order. For now, you want to see likenesses between parts and have a sense of the whole, without worrying about one idea following another in perfect time sequence.

Quieting the Critic

If you are having a block, you are probably not at a loss for words. Rather, words are getting in your way—mentally verbalized ideas such as, How can I fill this page? Am

I sure *this* idea wouldn't come before *that* idea? Is this sentence just right? Am I wasting my time? Will it be good enough? and on and on. There is no end to the words a writer can think up to keep herself from putting words on paper. She is blocked with words. She has let the dominant, verbal side of the brain use words to keep the subordinate, right side of the brain still. Yet the right side is the one that sees things as a whole and that has the unusual story to tell.

Since Roger W. Sperry and his associates at the California Institute of Technology did "split brain" studies and Betty Edwards, in the art world, popularized the left and right modes of the brain (*Drawing on the Right Side of the Brain,* Tarcher), most people are familiar with the idea that each side of the brain plays a different role. Whether or not you are concerned with which side of your brain is functioning, relaxing your mind so that you stop analyzing will help to free your creative powers. You must quiet the critic in you that judges a sentence to be inadequate before you can commit it to paper. Once the critic is asleep, the writer can gambol.

XX

Accurate Research

DOING accurate research is an important part of romance writing. You can prepare at home in several ways, so let's start there.

The Essential File

1. Travel. Collect pictures, articles, and travel folders about various cities and countries that appeal to you. Do the people wear special costumes? What are the local customs and events? What foods are eaten? What wines are drunk?

2. Housing Exteriors and Interiors. Subscribe to magazines that will give you material for your settings. Barbara Conklin draws floor plans of the houses in her young adult novels.

3. Pictures or Drawings. Clip pictures of those who would make interesting heroines or heroes. Conklin puts these by her typewriter.

4. Maps. Collect country and city maps with street names. I used a map of Regency London while writing *The Reluctant Duke.* I knew where some of the famous people of the time lived in relation to my characters.

5. Regional Food. Obtain delicious-sounding menus that would authenticate the setting. Meredith Kingston plans all the menus for her contemporary novels before she starts to write.

6. Ideas. If you have a clever thought or hear an entertaining anecdote, jot it down.

7. People. Take notes on people you've seen during the day. Did someone have an interesting way of walking or an unusual facial expression or mannerism? What outward signs indicated who they are underneath?

8. Incidents. What happened on a trip or outing that could be turned into a story? Take notes.

9. Friends' Notes. Have friends bring back material about their travels: the people, food, places, customs.

10. Clothes. Clip photos of costumes and daily wear from magazines, catalogues, etc., even lingerie for the characters.

11. Photographs. Take photographs as you travel. If possible, plan to visit spots that might later make good settings.

Presumably, not all these suggestions will be right for you. Let your interests guide you to the activities you'll want to pursue.

Leisure-Time Activities

Much of your leisure time can be used to help your writing career. Do you bowl? What about creating a mansion with its own bowling alley for your next story? How could a bowling game add conflict between the hero and heroine? Use what you know.

Attend travel movies (at which you will take copious notes) rather than the current popular film.

Subscribe to and read magazines that give you information about a variety of activities and that relate to your current topic, whether it's surfing or opera. If you want to try young adult romances, teen magazines can help you keep abreast of current teen trends. They also remind you of the problems young adults face.

Visit high schools. Talk to the students. Learn their interests, their fears, their desires.

Read one or two daily papers, clipping the articles and pictures that might later be just what you need.

Read what other authors are writing. Go to sleep each night with romance plots in your head.

Watch television, taking notes about how effects have been achieved. Think of how well *The Sound of Music, My Fair Lady,* and *Gone With the Wind,* three perfect romances, have done at the theater box offices. The *Thin Man* movies contain clever banter. Fred Astaire and Ginger Rogers always have cute meets.

Study how the actors portray a particular character. What does a good actor do to make you believe in a role? As you watch, don't forget to take notes. Think of how self-righteous you'll feel when you can attribute so much fine entertainment to hard work.

What other activities do you enjoy? Boat shows? The races? Swap meets? Always think of believable settings, using your own interests as a start.

Where To Turn for Help: Agencies, Collections, Individuals

1. Chambers of Commerce and Tourist Departments. Here you can learn where a particular restaurant is, and then you can write for the menu. You can ask about hills in San

Francisco and which streets are one-way only. You can discover what the department stores are in which your heroine might shop and where they are located. Once your story is underway, you will find you have specific questions about an area. Someone on the scene can help you.

Most governments have tourist information centers ready to help you. They can send you lists of hotels or maps or pictures as well as historical facts. Usually they are staffed by people from the area who can give you accurate information.

2. Consulates. These have an information service and can sometimes answer questions the tourist board cannot, such as titles for dignitaries or royalty and correct manners in certain situations. Consulates, too, are staffed by people from the area who know the answers to a variety of questions.

3. U.S. Government Agencies. The Federal Information Center, 601 East 12th St., Kansas City, MO 64106, (816) 374-2466, will let you know what government agency has the information you're seeking. When you write to the agency itself, be sure to ask specific questions.

The *Superintendent of Documents Catalogue* in your local library lists documents published by the government, and gives the price if there is one. The information covers a span of topics from diapers to atomic energy. Also available is the *U.S. Government Publications Reference File* on microfiche, which lists documents that are for sale.

4. Museums. Your local museum can help in many ways. The textile department can show you costumes from many periods and should have a good selection of books on the fashions of each period.

Paintings done in particular periods will give you an idea of not only the costumes and wigs, but also the wealthy, the poor, the military, houses, carriages, ships, roads, and canals.

Go to specialty museums: Indian crafts, Oriental art, antique cars, coins, furniture, or whatever. If you want to use Chinese paper-cutting or Indian weaving in a story, find out if your local museum teaches a class in what you need. For specialized information, a chat with a museum curator can be valuable.

5. *Interviews.* Talk to people who have lived in an area you're depicting. They can tell you facts that an outsider couldn't know.

6. *Old Mansions.* Most areas have restored houses that are famous. The docents and brochures can give you information you need. Pictures of the interiors and of the antiques can be invaluable in describing a setting.

7. *Antique Stores and Art Galleries.* For period pieces, you will want to become knowledgeable about antiques.

8. *Travel Agencies.* Your travel agent will supply you with folders and send for exact information.

9. *The Telephone Book.* Do you need to know time zones? Federal or state departments? The titles for city or county officials? You have them close at hand.

10. *Bookstores.* Shops that handle specialized and used books can help you locate copies of books out of print.

11. *Specialty Libraries.* Besides your public and university libraries, your city may have a medical library, a police department library, and a law library. Great collections, such as those in the Huntington Library in San Marino, California, or the William Andrews Clark Memorial Library in Los Angeles, may be housed near your area.

Libraries

Second homes for all writers are libraries. Here you will find fiction books, shelved alphabetically by the author's last name. However, don't completely trust fiction writers. Were they careful in their own research? How accurate a flavor of the period do they convey?

Nonfiction books can also be inaccurate. To be safe, *never use a fact until you have found it in two different sources.*

Don't hesitate to ask questions of the librarians. They can cut hours off your research time by knowing or finding the right material. A telephone call will often get your question answered. For instance, if you need a hard-to-locate book, your librarian will check the *Library of Congress National Union Catalogue* and be able to tell you what library in the country has a copy.

Let's take a hypothetical instance and see how we'd find the necessary material. Your editor wants a story set in or near Germany. We'll first turn to the card catalogue. Since it's a subject, author, and title file, we can look under our subject, Germany. Here we'll find subheadings; we choose "Description and Travel" and find books listed that give capsule views of German life—home, sports, festivals, etc. We check the dates of the material and try to use information that will not be dated.

In several of the books, we have found bibliographies. Since our branch library does not have a couple of books we need, we'll check the main library, making use of the interlibrary loan system. If necessary, we'll use a local university library. State universities are supported by you, and for a fee, you should be able to use the libraries.

We decide we are not concerned with history, since ours is a contemporary novel, and we do not want to get involved with politics. Now that we have selected our books, we turn to *The Readers' Guide* and check recent magazine articles. Under Germany, we find information on German cooking, the German Grand Prix, German opera, painting, pottery, wines, etc. The *Guide* suggests that we check under "Germany West": and we find more articles on ballet, banking, industry, education, dance festivals, etc.

We next check the *National Geographic Index*. Under "Germany" we find an article on the German Alps and even one entitled, "Down the Danube by Canoe." As we read, taking careful notes with the exact names of the magazine, article, author, and pages, we start favoring certain professions or interests for our characters, and definite locations. We decide to make our hero a great outdoorsman who loves mountain-climbing and skiing. The heroine will also be concerned with sports. She is an American (always, for American contemporary writers). She is a beauty. Let's have her race cars. But where can the two meet? Why not while hiking in Innsbruck, Austria? Then the hero must return to his home in West Berlin, since he is having trouble with an old knee injury. The heroine cannot go with him as he wishes because she's to be in a major auto race. She is getting acclaim in the sports world at a time when he, because of his knee, may never again be able to take an active part in sports.

Now we have specific information to check. We shall need to have some medical information about the problem with his knee. In the medical or sports section of the library, we look up knee injuries in the *Encyclopedia of Sports* (Macmillan, 1971). In the sports section, we check Macmillan's *Motor Sport Yearbook*. It may take hours of research before we are ready to outline our story.

Time for Research

In planning your writing day, leave time for research and reading. Avoid spending lumps of time, over a period of days or weeks, on research, then on writing. That way, you may not get to the writing. Be researching the next book while finishing this one, but be sure to write every day.

Researching a Period Piece

While working in a particular period, notice that language is constantly changing. The best way to learn what words were in use and how they were used is to read diaries, letters, journals, novels, plays, and poems written during the period. To check the meanings of words unfamiliar to you, go to the *Oxford English Dictionary (O.E.D.)*. In this work, you will find the various uses of that word from its earliest origins. If you want to employ a word and be sure that it had the same meaning in the past as it does today, check the *O.E.D.*

Introducing characters who actually lived in that period will make your story more believable and entertaining. Try to weave them into your tale as actual minor characters. Historic figures are included in a good general encyclopedia.

The characters from the period you're depicting lived on specific streets in houses of definite styles. Often you can visit such a house from the period. If not, you might find floor plans or pictures in books of the period. The characters shopped in stores of the time or checked books out of lending libraries. They attended theaters, parks, galleries, and other places of amusement. They may have traveled on particular vessels or in certain types of carriages.

People in past times acted according to social codes. What was the etiquette of the day? How were letters written? Books such as *The Art of Letter-Writing, A Manual of Polite Correspondence* (A.L. Burt, 1889), by Jennie Taylor Wandle, will give you clues about socially acceptable language and behavior.

In 1879, Marion Cabell Tyree edited *Housekeeping in Old Virginia* (John P. Morton). Here we find old family names, favorite recipes, and household hints, which tell us much about the period.

> Never let a servant take up ashes in a wooden vessel. Keep a sheet-iron pan or scuttle for the purpose. At night always have the water buckets filled with water and also the kettle, setting the latter on the stove or range, in case of sickness or any emergency during the night. Have kindling wood at hand also, so that a fire may be quickly made, if needed.

Your moment of danger could come from a fire in a wooden container, carelessly used by a servant.

A writer's research is never completed and is always fascinating to do. Facts learned will influence your plot, add color to your novel, and make the whole believable. (See

Appendix B for a list of books and periodicals that should be on your shelf next to your typewriter or word processor.)

If you are to be a professional writer, your life must change accordingly. You will think *writing* throughout your waking hours. Now, each thing you do will enrich your work as it enriches your life.

XXI

Checklist for a Tight Rewrite

REWRITING is the most important part of writing. The more carefully you write in the first place, the less rewriting you will have to do. Nevertheless, the time you take to go over your story will make the difference in whether or not it will sell.

Putting Your Manuscript Aside

If at all possible, put the manuscript aside for a time before you attempt to rewrite. The closer you are to the material when you go to revise, the less likely you are to be objective and catch mistakes. You should be far enough removed from the story to see that an incident lacks clarity or a character lacks definition. You will no longer remember what happens next and will notice if the plot doesn't progress smoothly. You will now be able to see if your hero and heroine are appealing and if their love scenes are plausible. If you can read your own work as if you were the reader, you will be more apt to do a good rewrite.

Proper Instruction

Don't read the manuscript to a friend unless that friend is a writer and you value his or her judgment. The friend may say it's wonderful when it isn't, and you will be on an ego trip instead of finding out what's wrong with your work. The friend may not like romances or may not like your particular romance, and you may become discouraged and put aside a salable work. If you need help, take a writing class and get sound, objective criticism. You wouldn't expect to play the violin without training. Writing is an art form, and is best developed with proper instruction.

If you do get help, remember that you don't have to agree with the criticism. It is your work, and you must be the final judge of what is right. But be open to the comments. Again, put the work aside, come back to it later with those comments in mind, and see if you agree.

When making corrections, if you use a typewriter rather than a word processor, use the cut-and-paste method. You will want to insert or move some passages. Simply snip your story in the appropriate spots, and use rubber cement to glue the pieces onto fresh white paper. This method allows you to Xerox the pages later without problems that could result from using tape or staples.

Those Helpful Rejection Slips

If you are lucky enough to get critical remarks from editors, save them, treasure them, and write thank-you notes. If you agree with the comments, do something about them. If not, think them out at a later date. When more than one editor makes a criticism, change that story. They know what will sell; and though they can be wrong, they are more often right.

One of the marks of a creative person is having faith in oneself; so if you think your story is just right, keep submitting it. Richard Bach, who wrote *Jonathan Livingston Seagull* (Macmillan), had trouble finding a publisher. Now his book is in print in over twenty languages, and was the first to be translated into Eskimo.

Reading Your Work Aloud

Before rewriting and after, read your story aloud. Pretend you are the characters. Are your lines natural and easy to say, or are they stilted? Would an actor want to play that part?

Listen for the unconscious repetition of a word. Hear any awkward structure. Listen to the dialogue in relation to the description. You will soon *hear* if you have included too much description.

The Courage To Cut

First, you will find you must do some cutting. There's an apocryphal story about the artist Rodin: When he was doing a sculpture of Balzac, attempting to show the stature of the great French writer, he sculpted powerful hands. Everyone who saw the sculpture praised the hands, so he cut them off. When asked why, he said they detracted from the work as a whole.

Keep this story in mind when you go to revise. No matter how magnificent a section of your novel is, if it does not add to the story as a whole, if it does not further the action, or characterization, it must now come out of your story. There, it will only distract and may cause some readers to put down the book.

A good rule to follow when cutting is that if you are unsure of a section and whether or not it works, take it out or completely rewrite it. Don't send off a manuscript with sections that are questionable in your own mind. Remember, your cutting is helping the reader to focus on what is essential; so the story will improve.

Reweaving

If you find your story is short, don't pad, though that will be your first temptation. First, check to see if you have all the necessary plot twists and sex scenes. If not, add a character or more plot convolutions. Rewrite the novel, weaving in the new character, thereby making the story stronger with contrasting and parallel situations. Don't neglect to do the reweaving. You can't just superimpose another character or incident.

Clichés

In category writing, the formula itself is a kind of cliché, so you must use fresh plot situations and fresh wording to compensate. Certain incidents have become clichés that some editors would like to avoid. The misunderstanding based upon the heroine's seeing the hero with another woman and jumping to the wrong conclusion is too fragile for a major disagreement. For me, the hero's raping the heroine and her adoring him afterwards has become a cliché, as has the drunk hero raping the heroine. I also think the wounded hero who can still make passionate love is unbelievable. Part of the fun of formula writing is to create new twists of plot.

The following lists should help you do a thoughtful, thorough rewrite:

Character Checklist

1. Do the hero and heroine meet early in the story, preferably on page one, with a major conflict? Is that conflict sexually oriented? Is the moment dramatic enough to be memorable?

2. Are the characters ones we want to identify with? Do we know enough about them to be sympathetic?

3. Is the problem between the hero and heroine one that is important enough to legitimately keep them apart, or is it a manufactured one that could easily be solved if one or the other merely mentioned it?

4. Do supporting characters help to move plot?

5. Is your hero a complex, haughty person? Have you avoided making him a philanderer or a playboy?

6. Is your heroine spunky, never showing self-pity or too much fear? Have you kept her from being cloyingly sweet?

7. Have you omitted, in most instances, serious illness or psychological problems for your characters?

8. Have you written from the heroine's point of view?

9. Have you let the characters tell their story with dialogue?

10. Does your dialogue suit your characters? Does it reveal character? Move the plot?

11. When the heroine finally realizes she loves the hero, is she certain he will never love her?

12. In the historical romance, soaps and sagas, do your characters experience deep emotion: guilt, rage, fear, doubt, pride?

13. Do the hero and/or heroine experience some character growth?

14. Is the love plausible and strong? Can we believe it will last forever?

Plot Checklist

1. Have you started your novel dramatically at a point of conflict rather than merely moving your heroine by some conveyance to the scene?

2. Have you used too many flashback scenes or started your novel with a flashback?

3. Does a fresh problem or a new slant to a continuing misunderstanding occur in each scene?

4. Is every scene vital to your story?

5. Are the misunderstandings, the obstacles to love, believable?

6. Are the sex scenes varied, and are they sensuous rather than explicit?

7. Have you avoided using coincidence or author manipulation to force events to happen your way?

8. Do you avoid clichés in wording or in plot situations?

9. Have you worked to a strong and satisfying climax?

10. Have you included a moment of danger?

11. Have you included a last-minute plot surprise?

12. Have you tied up all the loose ends in a satisfactory denouement?

13. Have you, except in a soap or saga, eliminated any social issues such as abortion, equal rights, use of nuclear power, or wilderness protection?

14. Have you omitted any reference to a timely event that could date your story?

Background Checklist

1. Have you omitted too much description of a room, food, clothes? Have you given enough?

2. Does your description fit in gracefully, or does it stop the story?

3. Does each detail you add serve a purpose in your story? Does your setting truly promote character and plot?

4. Do you intersperse description with dialogue rather than presenting it in chunks?

5. Do you appeal to the senses, drawing the reader into the scene?

6. In a period piece, do you use objects that are correct for the setting? Do the characters play the right sports, go to the right places? Have you really set your story in the past?

Style Checklist

Even if your plot, characterizations, and setting are excellent, style must be checked, if your story is to be a strong one.

1. Have you avoided using too many adjectives and adverbs?

2. Have you avoided repeating a word too often?

3. Do your verbs show action?

4. Are names dissimilar so that the characters cannot be confused?

5. Did you use the dictionary if you questioned the spelling or the meaning of a word?

6. If you changed a character's name, did you make the correction throughout the story?

7. Does each character have the same color eyes and hair at the end of the novel as at the beginning?

8. Have you varied the sentence structure?

9. Have you used the active, not the passive voice?

10. Have you varied the pacing?

11. Have you employed metaphor, symbolism, understatement, irony?

12. In a period piece, have you used the language of the period gracefully, or have you merely thrown in a few phrases to suggest the era?

A Final Check

Does your work flow when you read it aloud? Is the dialogue natural? Does one comment grow out of the preceding remark, unless the character is depicted as absent-minded or not listening? Are you pleased with the *sound* of your work?

Despite the formula, if you have something to say and feel it can be said only in a particular way, do so. All rules may be broken for a reason. It is often the book which stands apart that becomes a best seller.

After typing the final rewrite, scrupulously copyread the manuscript. You will pay to correct many errors once the galley proofs arrive. If you are satisfied, it is now time to get your story into the mail.

XXII

Successful Marketing

Romance editors do not insist on receiving manuscripts from agents, so you may choose to market your own work. For the first one or two novels, you might do better on your own, since an agent likes to see a "track record."

Manuscript Preparation

You will send Xerox copies, not the original, to romance editors. If you sell the manuscript, you will then send the original and one copy. Type on standard-size white bond paper, double-spacing and leaving margins of at least one inch on each side of the page, top and bottom. Use pica type, not elite or script. To figure word count, plan on 250 words to a page.

On the title page, in the upper left-hand corner, put your name, address, and telephone number. Opposite this information, on the right-hand side, put the approximate number of words in your manuscript. Editors expect you to keep to the number of words on their tip sheets. About one-third of the way down the page, center the title in upper case. Drop two spaces, tell the type of romance it is; drop another two spaces and center "by"; finally, drop two spaces and give your name. If you use a pseudonym under the title, be sure you have used your own name at the top of the title page and on each page thereafter. If you have already published a book, you may want to add at the bottom, "Author of," and give the title, publisher, and date your published work was released.

In case pages get separated, on each additional page put your name—not the title—in the upper left-hand corner. (You may want later to change the title or your pseudonym, and you won't want to correct every page.) Number the pages in the upper right-hand corner, starting with page two, and do not follow the numeral with a period or a dash. Double-space both manuscript and outline. Be sure that you correct all mistakes and never type over letters. Clean copy is easy to read and attractive to editors. When you Xerox the final draft, pay extra, if necessary, to get a perfect copy.

Never put a page in the typewriter without a carbon-copy sheet, preferably two or three. If you work on a word processor, make frequent copies of your tapes. Store the tape or carbon copy at another house or in the car. If a disaster should occur, don't run the risk of losing your work.

Your Nom de Romance

An author may use pseudonyms for several reasons. Some houses insist on a name they can develop that will be solely theirs. Some writers write different types of novels and don't like to confuse their readers. Men often do not want romance readers to know their identities. Writers might write books for money under one name, books for love under another.

Romance authors tend to use a different name with each house or line. Some have several pseudonyms, and finding these names takes careful sleuthing on the part of the reader. You can help your readers by making sure that the book is copyrighted under your own name, which will appear with the copyright information in the front of each book. Your book will be listed in *Books in Print* under your copyright name.

Careful thought goes into picking a nom de plume. Most writers aim at a name easy to remember. For my own nom de romance, I had two requirements. I wanted the first name to be somewhat unusual in America, and English to suit the Regency period. I wanted the surname to be easy to remember, yet regal. So I became Philippa Castle. Decide what you want your name to do for you. Now is your chance to be feminine, dramatic, what-you-will to suit your fancy or your material.

The Query

For romances, a query, or submission, consists of a cover letter, a synopsis or outline, and the first fifty pages.

1. The Cover Letter. In the cover letter, let the editor know why you have sent the manuscript to this line. If you have spoken to the editor, you can refer to the conversation. Here's a chance for you to play salesperson, indicating what that manuscript has to offer that house. Does your story have a novel setting? Does the heroine have an unusual occupation? Have you included a catchy plot twist? Realize that the editor has read hundreds of good romances and that you are undoubtedly not the first to come up with a particular idea, and don't go into detail. Briefly make a statement that will hook the editor. Let the editor know that you have something fresh to say, but do it in the fewest number of words.

Start your cover letter with a strong, direct opening paragraph, indicating in a nutshell what your story can contribute to that series.

In the second paragraph give your credits, if you have any. If not, briefly give your credentials. Don't tell the editor about all your travels. If your story is set in India and you lived there for a year so that your material is accurate and unusual, that is of interest. Any relevant personal experience can come into this letter. If your story is about a heroine who plays professional tennis and you're a tennis player, let the editor know. They key word is *relevancy*.

The final paragraph of your letter should tell exactly what is enclosed: a synopsis and three chapters, and a self-addressed, stamped envelope (SASE). Keep redrafting your cover letter until it is short and forceful.

The following is a sample cover letter:

Address
Date

Ms. Felicia Brown, Senior Editor
Heart of Love
Lance Publications
New York, New York 10017

Dear Ms. Brown:

I enjoyed hearing you speak at the Romance Writers' meeting in Los Angeles last month. After studying your tip sheet and reading your new line's three romances, I think you will like my novel *Wild Blows the Wind*, especially since you mentioned wanting a Gothic in a modern setting.

My story takes place during winter in a deserted mining town in California, where Megan, the heroine, wanders after an automobile accident. The plot depends heavily upon the weather itself to parallel the mood of terror.

Enclosed are the first three chapters along with a synopsis and SASE. I look forward to hearing from you.

Sincerely,

Letitia Tremble

Notice that Letitia has never sold a story or book, but that fact doesn't make her shy about writing a forceful letter. She has conveyed that she keeps up with her field; she has read the line; she has listened to what the editor wants, and she, too, has been thinking along those same lines; she has a good setting; and she knows about good writing techniques. Moreover, she has been brief.

2. *The Synopsis or Outline.* (See Chapter 6, "Developing Your Story," for suggestions on writing the outline.) This can be almost any length, from five pages on. Many writers prefer ten to twenty pages to get their story told adequately. This length also lets the editor know that the story has been thought through in detail. Be sure to tell exactly what happens to the characters at the conclusion. Editors aren't worried about the story being spoiled; they want to know how you intend to tie up every loose end.

3. *The First Fifty Pages.* Finally, you will enclose the first fifty pages of the manuscript or even half the manuscript if you are a new writer. Many editors want the entire manuscript from new authors; check the tip sheet for requirements. If you send the entire manuscript, you should still include the outline. You may number the outline pages in Arabic numerals, but do not number them as part of the manuscript.

Mailing the Manuscript

Mail your query in a manila envelope with a sheet of cardboard for protection. When you send the entire manuscript, put it in a box the size your typing paper comes in. A white box with a label containing your name and the name of the manuscript is less likely to get misplaced. In the lower left-hand corner of the envelope and on the stamped, self-addressed return envelope, print "Manuscript, Special 4th Class Mail."

Some houses send postcards to let you know your manuscript has arrived. Keep this card. The date the manuscript was received is important. An editor may take up to two months to read your work. If it takes longer, send a letter asking about progress. If you did not receive a card, you can check to see if your work did, in fact, arrive. Your letter should include the title of your novel and the date on which it was mailed by you or received by the house.

Literary Agents: Pros and Cons

Some literary agents specialize in the romance market, so finding an agent to handle your romance is not difficult. Finding the right one for you *is* difficult. You may first want to submit on your own to learn about marketing and to get a foothold.

If you want an agent, take some time to look around. Join local writers' groups and ask questions of the members.

What does the agent do? Supposedly, the agent works for the author while the editor works for the publisher. This arrangement creates a balance, with both author and publisher having representatives. In practice, however, agents often work for the publisher because this helps them to sell more books. An agent may not read your contract or may negotiate a weak one, counting on the quantity of manuscripts handled to make a sufficient return. A good agent will ask for changes in contracts where necessary and will keep the author's interests at heart. I find agents to be like the child in the nursery rhyme: when they are good, they are very, very good; and when they are bad, they are horrid.

The agent is your business agent, protecting your financial concerns. She or he is also your sales representative, knowing the best market for your manuscript. Finally, the agent is your literary critic, suggesting manuscript changes that will make your work more salable. Obviously, this is an almost impossible role to play, since several talents are required.

Could an agent harm you? Yes, by negotiating a bad contract, by not circulating your work or by sending it out too slowly, by not knowing the markets, by not knowing editors' immediate needs, and by giving you bad critical advice.

Some agents now ask for contracts with their writers. These can be helpful, spelling out exactly what is expected of each party. However, contracts can be difficult to break or put too great a load of the expense on the author. The beginning writer is apt to become so excited at the thought an agent will handle her, she will sign almost anything. The undesirable agent counts on this reaction.

Whenever you are presented with a contract, read it several times, and read it carefully. If it is a book contract, ask the editor questions. Study books such as Richard Curtis's *How to Be Your Own Agent* or Carol Meyer's *The Writer's Survival Manual: The Complete Guide to Getting Your Book Published* (see Appendix B). If you have joined writers' groups, someone in your group may be able to advise you. Contract attorneys are helpful, but your advance may not warrant the expense of an attorney.

Can an agent help you? Definitely. The right agent is invaluable. Ideally, he should be someone who understands your particular talent, will keep your best interests at heart, and will keep your spirits up, so you can get that next book written. This agent meets often with editors and knows their current needs. Romance editors are competing with several other houses, so on a moment's notice they may decide they want a certain locale, or no longer want a type of plot situation. The good agent is having daily conversations with editors and keeps up to date with their sudden whims. Yes, it is very helpful to have the marketing load taken off the writer, and it is lovely to have the encouragement and sound advice.

Relating to an agent is like a marriage of two minds that see writing in the same way. You may sign with several agents before you find just the right one. I think it's a good idea to wait and choose with caution. This is your career. You won't have a chance to do it over again.

Lists of authors' agents appear in *Writer's Market* in your local bookstore and in *Literary Market Place* in your main library. Check the date of your source to be sure the information is current.

Your Manuscript File

Keep a file folder for each manuscript. This will include a sheet or large card telling the manuscript's destination, including the publisher and editor, the date the manuscript was mailed, the cost of postage and return postage. If the manuscript is returned, mark the date, and make a brief note about the editor's response, if any. Then keep the correspondence, which will include the rejection slip, clipped to your carbon of the cover letter. If an editor sends a form rejection slip, that person isn't interested in your writing. If he or she signs the rejection slip, send in something else at a later date. If the editor writes you a letter, definitely do something else for that person. She or he likes your writing, but this piece wasn't suitable.

Your Tip-Sheet File

With your folder of tip sheets, be sure to have a card for each house, giving the editors' names and notes on any material you have about their preferences. If a different editor from the one to whom you sent your manuscript answers your letter, send your next manuscript to that person, and add the name to your file.

Multiple Submissions

Since most houses have slightly different formulas, it may be difficult to double-submit the same manuscript, especially in the contemporary category. Regencies, Gothics, and other period pieces are usually published by several houses at once; in that case, it is advisable to submit to more than one house at a time, letting the editors know you have made multiple submissions. How many houses should you submit to at one time? Any number you choose. The postage will be your limitation. Remember, however, that you may receive some critical comments that will cause you to wish you could rewrite before contacting other houses. For that reason, it's best to be judicious about the number.

Contracts

Even if you have a contract attorney, you should know as much as possible about reading a contract. The following are points to watch for in romance contracts.

Advances range from a thousand dollars to many thousands, depending upon the house and upon your track record. But remember, this is an advance against royalties. In other words, the advance will come out of what you will eventually earn on each book. A larger advance can mean that the publisher expects to sell more copies of your book. With romance series, standard numbers of a work are usually issued. Keep in mind that if the book stays in print, royalties will provide long-range earnings. Except for Harlequin Books, however, most romance publishers, especially those that issue series, do not reissue titles after the initial print run.

Some publishers buy the manuscript outright for a low flat fee, with no royalties or rights going to the author. I should advise against selling this way. It means you get no profits from further U.S. sales, no profits from foreign sales, and no profits from a film sale. You may want to sign such a contract to get a credit, but weigh the pros and cons carefully. As a professional, if you sign a bad contract, you are supporting a publisher who is working against the best interest of writers in general.

Some publishers give royalties but no foreign or movie rights. These publishers intend to push a big sale overseas, and you will see no profit from such sales. Try to get a percentage of these rights.

Some contracts give the editor a right to hire another author, at your expense, to do a rewrite if your own work is not satisfactory. Be sure you notice such a clause, and don't agree to it.

It's a good idea to have a clause in your contract authorizing only you to do any rewrites. Some romance editors think nothing of making changes in manuscripts, including adding sex scenes. Changes in writing style or additional unexpected passages could prove an embarrassment.

All contracts contain an option clause which says that the publisher has a right to the first chance at your next book, and sometimes at the same price. Try to get that clause omitted. If the book goes well, both you and the publisher will be happy to work together again. If it goes badly for you and you are not satisfied, you must go with this publisher again, and the new contract will contain the same clause. This publisher may offer you less than could another for your next book, which might be quite different in nature. Since the publisher can turn your work down, but you must let him have first chance at it, the clause is rather one-sided.

Know Your Markets

Whether or not you have an agent, you must know your markets so that you can aim your material. Check the magazine *Publishers Weekly* at your local library and watch for changes in established lines and changes in editors. Be sure to note new lines being added and find out their requirements.

If you are just starting out, spend hours in your local bookstore, studying what books each romance publisher produces. Admittedly, a category that is now for sale may be dying out behind the scene. Therefore, your next step is to find the editor's name by checking a current *Literary*

Market Place or *Writer's Market,* or by calling the publishing house and asking the switchboard operator. Then write and ask for a tip sheet. You will be told what material is needed.

To have a better chance at a quick sale, write the type of romance that more than one publisher is handling. Then you can multiple-submit or immediately send the manuscript out again if it is rejected.

Rejection Slips

Let me remind you again, rejections are a part of the writing job. You must learn to handle them well or pick another field. They are not necessarily a reflection on your ability. They could mean:

1. The publishing house is overstocked.

2. The editor is reading for two lines and has his or her mind on the other line that day.

3. The editor doesn't like your style. (That editor might also not like Hemingway's style.)

4. The house is contemplating phasing out this line and is no longer buying. You may not be told.

5. The editor has a family crisis or a headache or any number of problems that can color judgment.

6. The editor finds your topic distasteful. Your heroine could be superthin, and the editor's daughter suffers from anorexia nervosa.

7. The editor could be new to that line and resent some writers already picked by a former editor, preferring his or her own list of writers.

Revisions After a Sale

Sometimes writers forget that editors do edit. That can mean they want changes made after your manuscript has been purchased. If you disagree, you are free to say so, but the final judgment rests with the editor.

For instance, with *The Reluctant Duke,* I was asked to add more sex scenes. I discussed this change with the editor, reminding her that the duke was, after all, "reluctant." More sex scenes would mean changing the duke's character. We struck a compromise with my suggestion that I extend the existing sex scenes.

You *will* be expected to rewrite at the editor's request. Try to get a good reputation for doing prompt and thorough changes.

Always keep in mind that your editor knows what will sell. Her or his job is to make your story as readable as possible, thereby attracting more readers.

The Right Spirit

Your sale will be mostly from hard work—but hard work that you enjoy—some talent, and a large portion of luck. Many factors will be out of your control and will actually have nothing to do with you. Don't let these outer forces subdue your feelings about your talent. You had to have drive and ability to come this far. Don't be stopped by someone you don't know who presents a reason that might not be valid.

When submitting, think positively. Think sale. You have worked hard; and because of that work, your talent, and your tenacity, you will one day find an envelope with a contract inside.

XXIII

Publicizing Your Romance

T HE romance writer is in the relatively unique position of not really having to publicize her novel. Each month a publisher releases a certain number of romances. These books are distributed widely, a few to each store, depending upon location. Some stores have a sizable romance readership, others do not; and the books for chain stores are doled out accordingly. If the owner of the private bookstore errs, it will be on the side of fewer rather than more books, so that copies not quickly sold will not have to be returned. This means that the covers are torn off and sent back to the publishers so that the store can have a refund; and the books are shredded.

Romance books that reach the shelves are usually bought automatically by readers who follow that line or author. The books sell out fairly rapidly; and unless a demand is created for that particular title, which is unlikely, the books usually will not be reprinted.

You may want to take some steps on your own to get

your name and your story known. First, let's be sure what may be done on your behalf.

What the Publisher Will Do

How much promotion or publicity the publisher will undertake on behalf of your book depends upon the book itself. Some romance publishers buy big books and only a few of them. Such books will get more attention than will smaller romances, in a series. The publisher's money will be budgeted for each individual book according to the type of publicity that will probably be most effective: (1) ads in publications, (2) radio and television ads, (3) floor displays in bookstores and book departments, (4) posters, (5) bookmarks.

Are you an author who can be promoted? Some authors dislike appearing in public. Some do not make a good appearance. Most romance authors do not have an unusual angle for their material (see "On the Air," later in this chapter). As a novelist, you must be famous to attract an audience.

If your book is one of a series, the series itself is publicized on television and radio and in magazines. Galleys are sent to romance publications for review. A new series might promote individual authors in their own towns with local television and radio appearances, but on the whole, you are important to the publisher not as an individual author but as one in a group.

Avoiding False Expectations

The approximate sales you can expect for your book will be indicated by the size of the publisher's advance, which is calculated against royalties. Once you make a name for yourself, your advances rise because you have a following, resulting in more sales. Romances are not usually on the best-seller lists and individually do not earn large sums of money, so you should not have unreal expectations for your book. You will not get on national talk shows or radio shows or be in your city's leading newspapers because of an individual romance. Your book in itself does not mean big business. It takes many books to make your name known; therefore, don't waste your time and money competing where you won't do well.

What You Can Do

A number of activities will help you to make a local name for yourself and help sales of your book to a minor degree. Remember that the book will pretty much sell itself but that your publicity will advance the sale of future books. You are gradually building a career, and publicity is a major stepping-stone.

Writers' Organizations

Many romance writers have been helped along the way through joining writers' clubs at which they learn about the publishing world and hear talks from established writers. (See Appendix C for a list of writers' organizations.) You will find that getting down to work is a little easier after hearing about new markets or the success of other writers.

Organizations put out newsletters for their members. These newsletters are a good way to get your name into print and get your work known. If your group has a library, donate copies of your book.

Getting into Newsprint

If you are a relatively unknown writer, your best bet is to get into print in local papers and "throwaways." That is not necessarily easy. You will need to send a cover letter and a press release. The cover letter will sell you as news. You must include a "hook." Have you contributed to the community in some way? Is something about the book of special interest to those readers? Getting into columns about books or people is often better than a separate, brief article. The press release will be the article as you would wish it to appear. If it does not need rewriting, it is much more likely to appear. Be clean and precise, putting your facts in order of importance with the most important first, in inverted pyramid style. In the release, be sure to indicate who you are in relation to that area.

On each page, put your address and phone number—a number that can be reached. A newspaper must be sure of its sources and may call to check a point. Have available professional black-and-white glossy photographs, for you might need one on the spur of the moment. You may wish to send one with your press release. A good picture can help to get an article into print. Keep in mind that a photograph will not be returned to you. It is expensive, and there may be no return in sales for this type of expenditure.

Follow up to see if your article has appeared in print. Then keep the article on file. You will want to Xerox it later for your press or news kit. Many small publishers put out more than one newspaper. You might indicate in your cover letter which of their publications would have an audience for news about you.

Don't forget to contact your local college newspaper as well as the alumni magazine. You may belong to organizations other than writing groups that publish news about members.

If you write young adult romances, try to arrange an interview by local high school reporters. Send them a press release and a copy of your book.

Bookstores

Before your book is released, visit bookstores, introduce yourself, and let them know you will help to publicize your book. Ask how many copies they expect to receive.

Chain stores get orders determined in a central office, and many clerks don't care which books sell or even *if* books sell.

When your book is released, see that your book is visible in the bookstores and not buried under copies of someone else's novel. If you are the author of a "big," nonseries book, be sure your publisher has sent advance posters to bookstores throughout the country.

Ask to autograph store copies, and request bands that say "autographed by the author" to be put around the books. Autographed books tend to move, and the band calls attention to them.

Autograph Parties

New writers often eagerly await a chance to autograph their books. These "parties" are highly overrated. Unless you are very well known, and often if you are, you may sit fidgeting while the public passes you by. Bookstores have learned from experience that autographing parties often don't pay.

If you do have an autograph party, you will need large blowups of your book cover and large photographs of yourself. You will also need to check to see what the accommodations are. Will they remember to have a table and chairs, and will these be placed in a prominent position that will attract attention? Call six weeks in advance to see that the books have been ordered; then call to see if they have arrived.

Public Speaking

Public speaking is a fine way to get yourself and your novel known and to share ideas. If you are a novice at speaking, start practicing before a mirror. Get small groups of friends to listen to you. Ideally, take a class or join a Toastmasters' group.

Be available for talks in the community. Some libraries have book clubs at which you could appear. You might offer to review your own book.

Many women's groups have hefty budgets and, for their meetings, hire expensive entertainment from talent agents. Smaller clubs with low budgets would be thrilled at your offer to speak for little or nothing. When you're famous, you can command a large fee; at present, be glad to get the experience. Having a following among the women of your community may mean money from the royalties on future books. Senior citizen groups often appreciate meeting an author and hearing about her books.

Buy copies of your book from your publisher. You will want to give books away for publicity; and you must keep some on hand for future reference. You may be asked to send copies to another country for translation purposes, so be well supplied. Your book's life will be very short. Romances go out of print rapidly.

If you write young adult novels, your local public and private school librarians and English departments will be the spots to contact. Ask if you can talk to a group of students in the library at lunchtime. After school, teenagers have sports and other activities; school is a place to leave at three o'clock. Young people think of the writing profession as very romantic, and they will love to hear about how they might become writers. Offer to speak at the school's career days. If you do schedule a talk with students, notify the journalism class beforehand that you will be speaking, and give them a copy of your book.

Whenever you are scheduled to speak for an organization, check with the publicity chairman to make sure your PR efforts will not overlap. On the whole, don't trust the publicity person to do much, if anything. *You* send a notice to the calendar section of your newspaper. *You* put the date of the speech in your club newsletters. An exception occurs when you are conducting a seminar for a writing day or for some large group. In such an instance, you are not the only individual involved, and publicity should come from this organization.

The Press and News Kit

Local radio news stations and television stations may have shows on which you could be a guest. You can get lists of shows at the main branch of your library in *Television Contacts* and *Radio Contacts,* Larimi Communication Associates, Ltd., published yearly. This research guide gives the stations, the overall formats, the people involved, the programs, and what the station wants for programming. It is geographically arranged by state and city. Xerox the necessary pages.

You will need a press kit. It begins with a cardboard folder with pockets, one that you purchase in your local stationery store. Author and media consultant Anne Ready, creator of Ready for Media, Los Angeles, and past associate producer of ABC's top-rated local morning talk show, suggests that you make your kit stand out with an intriguing cover. "You might want to state the subject of your book: *She Never Understood the Man in Her Life;* or you might want to appear as an expert on romance, making a collage on the cover with a linen and lace handkerchief and a pair of theater tickets."

Inside the folder, you will first put a cover or "pitch" letter. This is your sales letter. It will include four or five points you can discuss and why these points will be of interest to listeners or viewers. Romances are similar because of the formula, so it is difficult for the media person to think, "Yes, this is just the person my audience must hear." Nevertheless, local shows may very well wish to feature a local author. "Writing romance novels is an excellent way to stay home with my children and still make some extra money," can be your pitch.

Next, insert a brief biography. Include points that relate to the book you're promoting.

You will then include Xeroxed copies of any articles that may have appeared about you in local papers. If you have none, ask yourself if you are doing enough about getting into print. Ready suggests that you include some articles about the importance of the romance genre, if you have nothing on your particular book.

Add a list of about ten possible questions the interviewer could ask. Chances are the book will never be read by the host, so pertinent questions will be valued.

Your newspaper "press release" becomes a "news release" for radio and television. And don't forget to send your picture and a copy of your book. Slip them into the pocket in front of the pitch letter.

On every page, picture, and book in your kit, put your name, address, and telephone number. These items are loose and can easily be separated. The kit will not be returned to you, so don't include return postage or ask for your book or picture back.

Once you have sent off the kit, your work isn't finished. In two or three weeks, follow up with a call asking what they think. You may have to do several follow-up calls about two weeks apart. When you call, you might suggest a new approach to the topic. There's a fine line between being assertive and aggressive, and you will be careful to be merely assertive.

The main thing to remember in sending a press or news kit is that the people involved don't care about your book. They care about their own ratings. They care about whether or not you have interesting information to impart to their listeners or viewers. Convince them that you do.

Tie-ins

If you are doing a television or radio show, be sure to let a local bookstore know, so that your book can be available. Books take up to six weeks to arrive, and you may not have that much notice. Ask the bookstore to request special handling and agree to mention the store's name as a place where the book can be purchased.

On the Air

You have been asked on a talk show because you have something to say, so don't answer with a yes or no; and don't depend on the list of questions you've given the moderator. They may or may not be followed, so prepare to be on your own. Los Angeles publicist Irwin Zucker reminds authors, "Read your book the night before, so that you will remember what it's about." The work in progress is usually the one uppermost in your mind. Zucker also suggests that you talk about your book every chance you get so it will be fresh in your mind.

If you are asked a question for which you don't have an answer, media consultant Ready says to give only a brief answer, then make a transition to something you do know. If you don't have any answer, you could say, "Yes, I think that's a popular point of view," or "Yes, I have heard that," or, "That's an interesting point." Follow this acknowledgment with a transition—"but," "however," "nevertheless"—then respond to what you do know or do want to say. No moderator will mind if you gracefully shift to something you can handle, thereby avoiding sin number one, the long pause.

"Have two or three salient points about your book in mind," says Ready, "and try to get these into the conversation no matter what turn it takes." You are selling your book, even if the moderator isn't.

The moderator will get ideas as he's talking, so be prepared for some surprises. He may decide to be controversial and let you represent all romance writers in defending the genre and its effects upon women. Anything can happen; expect the worst, so you won't be caught off guard and your experience can be a happy one.

Sin number two is rambling. Try to make your answers clear and concise.

Author and broadcast journalist Ciji Ware says, "If you are on the air, get tapes; if you are on television, have friends videotape the appearance. Be sure to have two peo-

ple record. Keep one tape; send the other to your publisher, proving how good you'd be on a national show."
Even for best sellers, start locally. Get practice.

Ready gives six points to help those going on a talk
show:

1. Know what you want to communicate.
2. Don't use the phrase "in my book." Instead, use the
book's title. Incorporate your title wherever you can in the
conversation.
3. Make the audience feel they are learning something.
People don't want to know about the characters in a novel.
They want practical advice. If they're watching a daytime
show, they want to justify taking the time to watch. Medical soap operas, for example, are the most highly rated
because women can justify learning about medicine. A
novelist has a problem in that she hasn't anything of an
informative nature to impart. So she should take the "how
to" approach. For instance, in Ready's appearances to discuss her own young adult romance, *Her Father's Daughter*
(Grosset & Dunlap Tempo), she stresses a girl's growing
up in a single-family household—how the daughter deals
with the single mother, what the daughter's needs are.
"The issue is actually incidental to the book as a whole,"
says Ready, "but the topic gives me a chance to impart
knowledge to the audience."
4. Don't oversell a book. You should give enough information to create excitement in yourself as a person and
in the subject. "The audience should be left feeling, 'Boy,
did I like her! I'd like to have her book.' "
5. If asked about a certain point, don't say, "Oh, that's
in Chapter 3," or, "If you had read my book, you'd know
the answer." Don't resent an uninformed host. He knows
as much about your book as the audience knows, and is
asking the questions they would ask.
6. When you get a question you *can* answer, compli-
ment the host: "That's an excellent question, Merv." You
have thereby accomplished two things: (a) you have used
the host's name and put yourself on a first-name basis with

him; (b) you have made the host feel good. If he is comfortable and happy, the interview will go well.

Romance writers could stress their own areas of expertise, using some theme that appears in their books. Ready suggests that any romance writer can be an expert on some phase of romance. "What do you do for your man to make him happy and responsive?" Having an area of expertise will help you to get on a talk show.

The Professional Publicist

Should you hire a professional publicist? Only if your book is expected to be a best seller and you have received a hefty advance. In that case, it will pay you to be seen, and keep that book on the top of the list. It will also behoove you to get to work on the next book instead of doing all the PR work yourself.

A good publicity campaign is expensive, sometimes costing in the thousands. Unless the publisher agrees to pick up the tab, you will pay for each city you go to, plus all expenses. Your publisher may agree to hire a PR firm for you. Usually, publicity is left up to the publisher's publicity department, and very little is done.

If you do decide you need a book publicist, how do you pick one? Publicist Zucker says, "Check with your local media people—radio and television." He reminds authors that once they have been given the name of a publicist, they should ask that publicist to furnish a list of satisfied customers. Zucker sees references as a must, comparing choosing a publicist to choosing a doctor. He is quick to point out, however, that the beginning author can do her own publicity.

Priorities

Doing your own publicity takes time. You must decide what your priorities are. How much time should be expended for what kind of return? The benefits for this one romance probably won't be significant, but building a following may help your career in the long run. Keep your overall career picture in sight. Publicity work is drawing from your writing time and energy. Would you do better to get that next book written and sold?

You should be able to budget some time for publicity, especially for speaking in the community. Besides gaining an audience, you can now contribute to those organizations that have brought you information in the past, and to your community in general. Encouraging other writers should have a high place on your list of priorities.

While publicizing your work or while writing, have a schedule that keeps you in focus. It's very easy to get started on publicity and forget to write. But a balanced approach with realistic expectations will result in a satisfying publicity experience.

Afterword

THE modern romantic heroine plays a dual role. She is the good wife, according to the standards of Western civilization; yet she is also the modern woman, affected by the feminist movement, who is able to branch out and show independence. Such a character is too ambiguous for some people to appreciate. However, she is a product of our society's approach to women.

I think that readers get a certain comfort in identifying, through romance literature, with both of these women—one from the past, the other looking toward the future. Women are not completely emancipated, and still define themselves in terms of past values. They are not ready to cast aside old norms, for these are the ways through which they have seen themselves. At the same time, they want more sexual freedom, better jobs, a chance to make more choices. They admire the spunky romance heroine who courageously strikes out on adventures, knowing she can handle any situation.

Caught between two opposite roles, today's women are uncomfortable. An escape into a fantasy world in which the heroine can handle the dichotomy and still get the man of her choice is one answer—a happy answer for readers and a lucrative one for publishers and romance writers.

Appendix A

ROMANCE PUBLISHERS AND THEIR LINES

Romance lines and editors are prone to change, but the following list is accurate as this book goes to press:

Avon Books, 959 Eighth Ave., New York, NY 10019. Page Cuddy, ed. Publishes mainly historicals and sagas.

Ballantine Books, 201 East 50th St., New York, NY 10022. Pamela Strickler, ed. Publishes historical and family sagas.

Love and Life series. Pam Strickler, ed. Heroine 28–45, torn between love and independence. Successful in career. American setting; glamour not necessary. Scenes not as sexy as an Ecstasy but couple goes to bed when in love. Story more realistic than in most other categories but with happy ending. Avoid mystery/ suspense plot, too much plot or too many characters, travel to foreign lands (may travel within U.S.). 50,000–60,000 words. Guidelines available.

Bantam Books, 666 Fifth Ave., New York, NY 10103. Linda Price, ed. Publishes historicals, Regencies, sagas.

Windswept Series. Carolyn Nichols, ed. Contemporary with three lines under umbrella title: (1) Heroine 18–23, virgin entering life, may be in school or trade school; "love, tender and thrilling." (2) Heroine 24–35, in full swing; "love, beautiful and blazing." (3) Heroine 35–45; "love, rich, ripe, wonderful." High degree of sensuality; credibility of character, setting, plot. Humor lightens. Avoid clichés, lapses in point of view. 55,000–60,000 words.

Young adult, *Sweet Dreams* series, Ron Buehl, ed. Screened by Cloverdale Press, 133 Fifth Ave., New York, NY 10003. Heroine 16, hero 2 years older. Tender story of first love. 45,000–50,000 words. Guidelines available.

Berkley/Jove, 757 Third Ave., New York, NY 10017. Beverly Lewis, ed. Publishes contemporaries and historicals.

Second Chance at Love series, Ellen Edwards, ed. Heroine 24–34, American, in fairly high-level job. Hero 5 to 8 years older and successful. Exotic foreign settings preferred, with no reference to a date in history. First love is past; divorce papers are signed. Sex after couple is in love. Avoid plots built around child, brittle glamorous other woman, adultery, Gothic elements. 60,000 words. Guidelines available. Some Second Chance Regencies.

To Have and To Hold series. Ellen Edwards, ed. Couple are married when book opens. The two are in conflict during course of story but stay together, reaching a deeper commitment. Depicts marriage as fun, adventurous, enriching, exciting, though not without problems; a relationship that is, above all, romantic. Plot situations are more realistic, more mature. 60,000 words. Guidelines available.

Young adult, *Caprice* series. Betty Ann Crawford, ed. 200 Madison Ave., New York, NY 10016. Heroine 15–16, hero 16–17. Girl's emotions first bloom in the relationship. Strong supporting characters. 50,000–60,000 words. Guidelines available.

Dell Publishing Co., 245 East 47th St., New York, NY 10017. Kathy Sagan, ed. Publishes sagas, soaps, historicals.

Candlelight Ecstasy series. Anne Gisonny, ed. Heroine 25–35, established career. U.S. settings. Heroine and hero meet on equal terms; both are mature, intelligent, sophisticated. Love scenes extensive, sensuous, provocative. Plot complications emerge from emotional involvements of characters. Avoid contrived or coincidental circumstances, a sweet style. 50,000–60,000 words. Guidelines available.

Doubleday Publishing Co., 245 Park Ave., New York, NY 10167. Veronica Mixon, ed. *Starlight Romances,* hardcover series. Goes mainly to schools and libraries. Modern, historical, Regency, ethnic. Heroine in 20s or early 30s. Tender love scenes, light petting and kissing only. Avoid romantic suspense. 70,000 words. Guidelines available.

E. P. Dutton, 2 Park Ave., New York, NY 10016. Young adult, *Starlight Romances Book Club,* Kathy O'Hehir, ed. Heroine 16; hero a year or two older. High school or vacation settings. Strong conflicts. Lighthearted romances appreciated. 35,000 words.

Fawcett Books, now owned by Random House, 201 East 50th St., New York, NY 10022. Kathy Repetti, ed. One Regency (including series historicals) every other month. 55,000 words. Fawcett Crest list is 95% reprints.

Harlequin Books

Canada: 225 Duncan Mill Rd., Don Mills, Ontario, Canada M3B 1X3. *Superromance* series. Star Helmer, ed. More sophisticated contemporary plots with subplots. Sensuous love scenes stressing shared experience rather than male's domination. Exotic settings. 90,000 words. Guidelines available.

New York: 919 Third Ave., New York, NY 10022. *North American* line. Vivian Stephens, ed. Heroine 25 or older, typifying average middle-class American woman. Hero, any age compatible with heroine; an achiever, though needn't be rich or "on top." Sex appeal more important than good looks. Point of view basically heroine's, but he can have a voice. American settings. 70,000–75,000 words. Guidelines available.

London: Mills & Boon, Brook's Mews, London WIA IDR, England. *Harlequin Presents* series. Jacqui Bianchi, ed. Heroine young, hero older. Characters lovingly portrayed through action, not description. Sex well integrated with story. Major love scene near climax. Happy-ever-after but not cloying. 55,000 words. *Harlequin Romance* series, similar to *Presents* in basics but with gentler romance. 55,000 words.

The New American Library, 1633 Broadway, New York, NY 10019. Hilary Ross, ed. Publishes sagas, Regencies, historicals.

Adventures in Love series. Robin Grunder, ed. Youthful heroine with sense of maturity in goals. Older hero. Adventure with gentle romance. Setting national or international, exotic or realistic.

Avoid tragic events, elements of mystery and suspense. 55,000 words. Guidelines available.

Rapture series. Robin Grunder, ed. Heroine youthful but with sense of maturity. Hero older and successful, not necessarily wealthy or athletic. Very sensual, adult situations. In competition with Silhouette *Desire* and Dell *Ecstasy* lines. 55,000 words. Guidelines available.

New series (as yet unnamed). Robin Grunder, ed. Heroine and hero over 35. Lushly romantic. Excitement at first encounter. Mutual pledge of undying love. Their lives enhanced by romance, not saved by it. Hero successful and athletic; treats heroine as equal, though he may clash with her. After definite courting period and mutual commitment, couple make love. Avoid rape, use of alcohol. 55,000 words. Guidelines available.

Young adult, *Signet Vista* series. Cindy Kane, ed. No one type of romance for this line. Focus is on development of heroine's character as well as her first romantic relationship. Small touches of humor appreciated. 50,000–60,000 words. Guidelines available.

Parents Magazine Press, 52 Vanderbilt Ave., New York, NY 10017. Young adult, *Fantasy Romance* series for paperback romance club. Stephanie Camenson, ed. Heroine 15–16, hero 17–18. Realistic problems but upbeat ending. Heroine grows to better understand herself. 45,000–50,000 words. Guidelines available.

Scholastic Book Services, 50 West 44th St., New York, NY 10036. Ann Reit, ed. Young adults.

Wildfire series. Heroine 15–16, hero 17–18. The realistic problems of a young girl in her first or early romantic relationship. 40,000–45,000 words. Guidelines available.

Windswept series. Heroine 16–17, hero 18–20. Gothic line about *real* girl (not Gothic type) who gets involved with frightening happenings. One plot line and a strong romance line. 40,000–45,000 words. Guidelines available.

Wishing Star series. Heroine 15–16, hero 17–18. High school students. Plots deal with problems like school difficulties, loneliness, death, parental difficulties, divorce. Avoid sexual matters like abortion, pregnancy. 40,000–45,000 words. Guidelines available.

Simon & Schuster, 1230 Ave. of the Americas, New York, NY 10020. Pocket Books, *Tapestry* series, Kate Duffy, ed. Shorter historicals (75,000 words) that stress romantic aura instead of rapes and violence.

Silhouette Romance series. Karen Solem, ed. Traditional, Harlequin-type romance set mainly in U.S. 55,000 words. Guidelines available.

Silhouette Special Edition series. Karen Solem, ed. Heroine 23–29, intelligent, accomplished, mature. She need not be a virgin and may be divorced (not her fault). Hero 8 to 12 years older, successful, not always conventionally handsome. He may be widower or divorcé, but both are single when they meet. Premarital lovemaking acceptable. Minor characters important and realistic, often bring out aspects of hero and heroine that haven't been evident in their relationship. Plots complex and believable with subplots that parallel or contrast with main plot. 70,000–75,000 words. Guidelines available.

Silhouette Desire series. Karen Solem, ed. Heroine in her 20s, mature and capable, not necessarily American. Hero a realistic modern man, American or foreign, mid- to late 30s. Both international and U.S. romantic locales. Plot centers on love relationship, with evocative descriptions of lovemaking (exotic sensations rather than mechanics). Emphasis on realistic problems and doubts of the modern woman. "A celebration of the physical pleasures of love as well as its emotional side." 50,000–55,000 words. Guidelines available.

Young adult, *Silhouette First Love* series, Nancy Jackson, ed. Heroine 15–17, hero a year or two older. Tension involves her romantic fantasies as opposed to reality, her need to define herself, and her common adolescent problems. Strong supporting characters. 50,000–60,000 words. Guidelines available.

Warner Books, 75 Rockefeller Plaza, New York, NY 10020. Kathleen Malley, Fredda Isaacson, editors. Historicals, contemporaries, sagas. Well scheduled for next few years, so only looking at "big" books (quality and length—approximately 160,000 words).

Zebra Books, 475 Park Ave. S., New York, NY 10016. Pesha Finkelstein, ed. Publishes historicals, Gothics, sagas. Heroine has only one love—the hero. Love scenes consummated. Rape scenes are with hero, *not* villain. Hero and heroine must eventually marry. Heroine may get pregnant before marriage. 125,000 words.

Leather and Lace series. Leslie Gelbman, ed. Combination historical and Western. Based on fact or legend; focus is on a famous woman who rode the West or who helped a famous man tame the West. They need not marry or even give a commitment, but ending must be upbeat. Love, romance, adventure, sex, and descriptions of homes, clothing, scenery. 75,000 words. Guidelines available.

Appendix B

RESOURCE WORKS FOR YOUR HOME LIBRARY

A number of books should be on your shelf next to your typewriter or word processor. The following are some you might consider.

1. *A Manual of Style, Revised, for Authors, Editors, and Copywriters,* University of Chicago Press, Thirteenth Edition. This book goes into the fundamentals of bookmaking and is a how-to guide for authors and editors. The chapter on rights and permissions reflects the new laws, and that on the new technology shows the impact of modern trends on the entire publishing process. Editors use this book for questions on style and so should you.

Important to the new writer is the list of proofreaders' marks with an example of marked proof. You will receive the galley proofs of your book once it has been printed, and you will want to return these with the proper correction symbols.

2. *The Compact Edition of the Oxford English Dictionary,* Oxford University Press. This is an unabridged dictionary in two photo-reduced volumes, with a magnifying glass for reading. You will use it to trace a word etymologically.

3. *Webster's Seventh New Collegiate Dictionary,* edited by Philip B. Gove, G. & C. Merriam Company. Based on *Webster's Third Interna-*

tional Dictionary, which is unabridged, this smaller version gives 130,000 vocabulary items and 10,000 usage examples. This, too, contains proofreaders' marks and a style handbook.

4. *Webster's New World Dictionary, Second College Edition,* edited by David B. Guralnik, Simon & Schuster. Some writers prefer this as a source to *Webster's Seventh* because of the number of synonyms, plus some antonyms. This, too, gives style samples for various types of writing.

5. *Roget's Thesaurus of English Words and Phrases,* by Peter Mark Roget, Thomas Y. Crowell. If you need to look up synonyms, this book is for you. It will help you use variety in wording and will save you time when you're searching for that right word. This is a key word index, arranged by categories.

6. *Writer's Market,* Writer's Digest Books, Cincinnati, Ohio, updated on a regular basis. A marketing book is a must if you intend to act as your own agent. It lists and describes the activities of every type of publisher, and it gives a list of literary agents and their services. Writers' groups are listed as are contests and awards.

7. *A Writer's Guide to Book Publishing,* by Richard Balkin, Hawthorn/Dutton. This reference work tells how an editor evaluates a manuscript, how to make a proposal, and how to negotiate a contract.

8. *The Writer's Survival Manual: The Complete Guide to Getting Your Book Published Right,* by Carol Meyer, Crown Books. The author, former managing editor at Harcourt Brace Jovanovich, includes advice about permissions, subsidiary rights, and book clubs. She answers questions authors often ask her.

9. *How to Get Happily Published,* by Judith Appelbaum and Nancy Evans, Harper & Row. This guide is packed with information from "Evaluating Manuscript Evaluations" to "Sales Strategies." It has excellent lists of resources.

10. *How to Be Your Own Agent,* by literary agent Richard Curtis, Houghton Mifflin. Curtis takes up contracts, author-publisher relations, royalty statements, and much more.

11. *Characters Make Your Story,* by Maren Elwood, The Writer, Inc. Elwood shows the writer how to select traits that individualize, how to handle both static and dynamic characterization, dialogue, thoughts. The chapter on developing plot from character will be of special interest to romance writers.

12. *Modern Fiction Techniques,* by F. A. Rockwell, The Writer, Inc. A teacher of writing, Rockwell tells how to write what will publish.

13. *Structuring Your Novel: From Basic Idea to Finished Manuscript,* by Robert C. Meredith and John D. Fitzgerald, Barnes & Noble Books. With clear examples, the authors take you through the phases of organizing and developing your material.

14. *The Creative Writer's Handbook: What to Write, How to Write It, Where to Sell It,* by Isabelle Ziegler, Barnes & Noble Books. This

handbook gives step-by-step guidance and includes end-of-chapter exercises.

15. *Writing Juvenile Stories and Novels,* by Phyllis A. Whitney, The Writer, Inc. Whitney tells how to approach material from the young person's point of view. She presents many clever "how to" ideas, showing ways to use technique to avoid problems.

16. *The Elements of Style,* by William Strunk, Jr., with revisions, and introduction, and a chapter on writing by E. B. White. Macmillan Publishing Co., Third Edition. In few words, this classic little book tells the author how to write lucid prose.

Magazines and Newspapers

A variety of magazines and newspapers on the romance are available and will help to keep you up to date on trends and on books others are writing. Several that have proved popular are (1) *Affaire de Coeur,* 5660 Roosevelt Pl., Fremont, CA 94538; (2) *Romantic Times,* 163 Joralemon St., Suite 1234, Brooklyn Heights, NY 11201; (3) *Boy Meets Girl,* Rainy Day Books, 2812 West 53rd St., Fairway, KS 66205; (4) *Barbara's Critiques,* 2710 R.D. Mize Road, Independence, MO 64057; (5) *Heart Line,* 140 Schoolhouse Lane, Brookhaven, PA 19015; and (6) *Romance Books and Reviews,* 3744 Charlemagne, Long Beach, CA 90808.

A must for romance writers in understanding the publishing world is *Publishers Weekly,* R. R. Bowker Co., Circulation Dept., 1180 Avenue of the Americas, New York, NY 10036. Through this periodical you will get publishing news in advance and be prepared for new lines coming onto the market.

Two magazines dealing with the craft of writing are: (1) *The Writer,* The Writer, Inc., 8 Arlington St., Boston, MA 02116; and (2) *Writer's Digest,* Subscription Dept., 205 West Center St., Marion, OH 43306. Reading articles by others who ply your craft can help you to improve and can be encouraging.

Appendix C

WRITERS' ORGANIZATIONS

Romance Writers of America, national with local chapters, 5206 FM 1960 West, Suite 208, Houston, TX 77069. *Romance Report* keeps members informed about the romance field and about members' activities. At a yearly June conference, writers, editors, and agents gather for workshops.

Women's National Book Association, national with local chapters, P.O. Box 237, FDR Station, New York, NY 10150. Both men and women book lovers as well as those working in publishing and related fields meet to learn more about books and the world of publishing.

Mystery Writers of America, national with local chapters, 150 Fifth Ave., New York, NY 10011. Many mystery writers also write romantic suspense or adventure stories. MWA boasts such members as Patricia Matthews and Phyllis A. Whitney. Monthly meetings and a newsletter keep members informed. A yearly convention presents "Edgar" awards to top mystery writers.

The Society of Children's Book Writers, national, P.O. Box 296, Mar Vista Sta., Los Angeles, CA 90066. Authors writing young adult romances will want to be part of this group that puts out a newsletter and presents a four-day conference each August in Santa Monica, CA.

P.E.N., national with local chapters, American Center, 47 Fifth Ave., New York, NY 10003. Besides producing a variety of publications such as a list of grants for writers, P.E.N. is dedicated to a free press in all nations. Two published books are required for membership.

Works Cited

Alexander, Serena, See Ramirez, Alice.

Ashton, Violet. *Love's Rebellious Pleasure*. New York: Fawcett Books, 1978.

————. *Love's Triumphant Heart*. New York: Fawcett Books, 1977.

Austen, Jane. *Pride and Prejudice*. 3 vols. London: T. Egerton, 1813.

Bach, Richard. *Jonathan Livingston Seagull*. New York: Macmillan Publishing Co., 1970.

Bancroft, Iris. *Rapture's Rebel*. Los Angeles: Pinnacle Books, 1980.

Bonds, Parris Afton. *Dust Devil*. New York: Fawcett Books/Popular Library, 1981.

Bowen, Elizabeth. *The Death of the Heart*. 2d ed. New York: Vintage Books, 1958.

Bradley, Muriel. *Tanya*. New York: Richard Gallen Books, 1980.

Brontë, Anne [Bell, Acton]. *The Tenant of Wildfell Hall*. 3 vols. London: Thomas Cautley Newby, 1848.

Brontë, Charlotte [Bell, Currer]. *Jane Eyre: An Autobiography*. 3 vols. London: Smith, Elder and Company, 1847.

Brontë, Emily [Bell, Ellis]. *Wuthering Heights*. 2 vols. London: Thomas Cautley Newby, 1847.

Brown, Sandra [Ryan, Rachel]. *Eloquent Silence.* New York: Dell Publishing Co., Candlelight series, 1982.

Brucker, Meredith Babeaux [Lindley, Meredith]. *Against the Wind.* New York: Silhouette Romances, 1981.

———— [Kingston, Meredith]. *Aloha, Yesterday.* New York: Jove Publications, Second Chance at Love series, 1981.

———— [Kingston, Meredith]. *Winter Love Song.* New York: Jove Publications, Second Chance at Love series, 1981.

Burford, Lolah. *Edward, Edward.* New York: Macmillan Publishing Co., 1973.

Cartland, Barbara. *Touch a Star.* New York: Jove Publications, 1981.

Castle, Jayne. See Krentz, Jayne.

Castle, Philippa. See Lowery, Marilyn M.

Clay, Rita. See Estrada, Rita Clay.

Coleridge, Samuel Taylor. "Kubla Khan." In *The Poetical and Dramatic Works of S. T. Coleridge,* Vol. I. Boston: Little, Brown & Co., 1854.

Conklin, Barbara. *P.S. I Love You.* New York and Toronto: Bantam Books, Sweet Dreams series, 1981.

———— *The Summer Jenny Fell in Love.* New York and Toronto: Bantam Books, Sweet Dreams series, 1982.

Coward, Noel. *Blithe Spirit.* New York: Doubleday, Doran, and Company, 1941.

Cukor, George, dir. *My Fair Lady.* With Rex Harrison and Audrey Hepburn. Warner Brothers, 1964.

Curtis, Sharon, and Curtis, Thomas Dale [London, Laura]. *The Bad Baron's Daughter.* New York: Dell Publishing Co., Candlelight Regency series, 1978.

Dailey, Janet. *This Calder Sky.* New York: Pocket Books, 1981.

Day, Jocelyn. See McCourtney, Lorena.

De Blasis, Celeste. *The Night Child.* New York: Coward, McCann & Geoghegan, 1975.

———— *The Proud Breed.* New York: Coward, McCann & Geoghegan, 1981.

———— *The Tiger's Woman.* New York: Delacorte Press, 1981.

Devereaux, Jude. See White, Jude Gilliam.

De Zavala, Marisa. See Mullan, Celina Rios.

Du Maurier, Daphne. *Rebecca.* Garden City, N.Y.: Doubleday and Company, 1938.

Dunnett, Dorothy. *The Game of Kings.* New York: Fawcett Books, 1961.

Edwards, Betty. *Drawing on the Right Side of the Brain.* Los Angeles: J. P. Tarcher, 1979.

Estrada, Rita Clay [Clay, Rita]. *Wanderer's Dream.* New York: Silhouette Books, 1981.

Fleming, Victor, dir. *Gone With the Wind.* With Clark Gable and Vivien Leigh. MGM, 1939.

Galsworthy, John. *The Forsyte Saga.* New York: Charles Scribner's Sons, 1961.

Gellis, Roberta. *Winter Song.* New York: Playboy Press, 1982.

Goldsmith, Oliver. *She Stoops to Conquer or, The Mistakes of a Night.* London: F. Newberry, 1773.

Graham, Winston. *Demelza: A Novel of Cornwall, 1788–1790.* The Bodley Head, 1976.

Granbeck, Marilyn. *Maura.* New York: Jove Publications, 1979.

Hager, Jean. *Portrait of Love.* New York: Dell Publishing Co., Candlelight Ecstasy series, 1981.

Hardy, Thomas. *The Return of the Native.* New York: Harper and Brothers, 1895.

Heyer, Georgette. *Cousin Kate.* 2d ed. New York: Fawcett Crest, 1968.

——— *The Nonesuch.* 2d ed. New York: Fawcett Crest, 1962.

Hohl, Joan [Lorin, Amii]. *The Tawny Gold Man.* New York: Dell Publishing Co., Candlelight Ecstasy Series, 1980.

Holland, Sheila [Lamb, Charlotte]. *Duel of Desire.* 2d ed. Toronto: Harlequin Books, Presents series, 1979.

Holt, Victoria. *The Legend of the Seventh Virgin.* New York: Doubleday, 1965.

——— *Shivering Sands.* New York: Doubleday, 1969.

Huxley, Aldous. *Crome Yellow.* New York and London: Harper and Brothers, 1922.

Jackson, Angela, and Opoku, Sandra Jackson [Sanders, Lia]. *The Tender Mending.* New York: Dell Publishing Co., Candlelight Ecstasy series, 1982.

James, Henry. *The Golden Bowl.* New York: Charles Scribner's Sons, 1904.

Karron, Kris. See Norris, Carolyn.

Kingston, Meredith. See Brucker, Meredith Babeaux.

Krentz, Jayne [Castle, Jayne]. *Gentle Pirate.* New York: Dell Publishing Co., Candlelight Ecstasy series, 1980.

Lamb, Charlotte. See Holland, Sheila.

Lambert, William III [Lambert, Willa]. *Love's Emerald Flame.* Toronto: Harlequin Books, Superromance series, 1980.

Lawrence, D[avid] H[erbert]. *Lady Chatterley's Lover.* New York: Grove Press, 1957.

_____ *The Plumed Serpent.* New York: Alfred A. Knopf, 1972.

Lester, Samantha. See Roper, Lester.

Lindley, Meredith. See Brucker, Meredith Babeaux.

Lindsay, Rachel. *Castle in the Trees.* 2d ed. Toronto: Harlequin Books, Presents series, 1974.

London, Laura. See Curtis, Sharon and Thomas Dale.

Lorin, Amii. See Hohl, Joan.

Lowery, Marilyn M. [Castle, Philippa]. *The Reluctant Duke.* New York: Dell Publishing Co., Candlelight Regency series, 1981.

Mansfield, Elizabeth. See Schwartz, Paula.

Matthews, Patricia. *Love's Avenging Heart.* Los Angeles: Pinnacle Books, 1977.

McCaffrey, Anne. *Ring of Fear.* New York: Dell Publishing Co., 1971.

McCourtney, Lorena [Day, Jocelyn]. *Glitter Girl.* New York: Jove Publications, Second Chance at Love series, 1981.

Michel, Freda. *The Machiavellian Marquess.* 2d ed. New York: Fawcett Crest, 1977.

Mitchell, Margaret. *Gone With the Wind.* New York: Macmillan Publishing Co., 1936.

Mullan, Celina Rios [de Zavala, Marisa]. *Golden Fire, Silver Ice.* New York: Dell Publishing Co., Candlelight Ecstasy series, 1981.

Norris, Carolyn. *A Feast of Passions.* New York: Pocket Books, 1980.

_____ , Carolyn Brimley. *Island of Silence.* New York: Popular Library, 1976.

_____ [Karron, Kris]. *The Rainbow Chase.* New York: Richard Gallen Books, 1981.

Peck, Richard. *Amanda Miranda.* New York: The Viking Press, 1980.

Peyton, K. M. *The Edge of the Cloud.* Cleveland and New York: The World Publishing Company, 1969.

_____ *Flambards.* Cleveland and New York: The World Publishing Company, 1967.

Pollowitz, Melinda. *Princess Amy.* New York and Toronto. Bantam Books, Sweet Dreams series, 1981.

Preble, Amanda. See Tayntor, Christina B.

Quinn, Alison. *The Satyr Ring.* New York: Harlequin Books, forthcoming.

Radcliffe, Ann. *The Mysteries of Udolpho.* 4 vols. London: G. G. and J. Robinson, 1794.

Ramirez, Alice [Alexander, Serena]. *Rapture Regained.* New York: Jove Publications, Second Chance at Love series, 1981.

Ramstetter, Victoria. *The Marquise and the Novice.* Tallahassee, Fla.: The Naiad Press, 1981.

Ready, Anne Cooper. *Her Father's Daughter.* New York: Grosset & Dunlap, Tempo series, 1981.

Receveur, Betty Layman. *Molly Gallagher.* New York: Ballantine Books, 1982.

Richardson, Samuel. *Pamela: or Virtue Rewarded.* 4 vols. In *Novelist's Magazine,* Vol. XX. London: Harrison and Company, 1786.

Rogers, Rosemary. *Wicked Loving Lies.* New York: Avon Books, 1976.

Rome, Margaret. *The Girl at Dane's Dyke.* 2d ed. Toronto: Harlequin Books, Romance series, 1976.

Roper, Lester [Lester, Samantha]. *Love's Captive.* New York: Dell Publishing Co., Candlelight Regency series, 1979.

Rostand, Edmond. *Cyrano de Bergerac.* Translated by Brian Hooker. New York: Henry Holt and Company, 1937.

Ryan, Rachel. See Brown, Sandra.

Sandburg, Carl. "Fog." In *Modern American Poetry.* Edited by Louis Untermeyer. New York: Harcourt, Brace, and Company, 1950.

Sanders, Lia. See Jackson, Angela and Opoku, Sandra Jackson.

Sargent, John Singer. *Doctor Pozzi at Home,* 1881. Los Angeles County Museum of Art.

Schwartz, Paula [Mansfield, Elizabeth]. *The Phantom Lover.* New York: Berkley Publishing Corp., 1979.

Seale, Sarah. *The Unknown Mr. Brown.* Toronto: Harlequin Books, Romance series, 1972.

Sheridan, Richard Brinsley. *The Rivals* and *The School for Scandal.* New York: Heritage Press.

Sitwell, Edith. "Aubade." In *Modern British Poetry.* Edited by Louis Untermeyer. New York: Harcourt, Brace and Company, 1950.

Spencer, LaVyrle. *The Endearment.* New York: Richard Gallen Books, 1982.

———. *The Fulfillment.* New York: Avon Books, 1979.

Steel, Danielle. *Season of Passion.* New York: Dell Publishing Co., 1979.

Stratton, Rebecca. *Isle of the Golden Drum.* Toronto: Harlequin Books, Romance series, 1976.

Tayntor, Christina B. [Preble, Amanda]. *Half Heart.* New York: Dell Publishing Co., Candlelight Romance series, 1981.

Thoreau, Henry. *A Week on the Concord and Merrimack Rivers.* New York: Thomas Y. Crowell Co., 1961.

Thorpe, Kay. *Lord of La Pampa.* 2d ed. Toronto: Harlequin Books, Presents series, 1978.

Tyree, Marion Cabell. *Housekeeping in Old Virginia.* Louisville, Kentucky: John P. Morton and Company, 1879.

Van Dyke, W. S., dir. *The Thin Man.* With Myrna Loy and William Powell, MGM, 1934.

Van Slyke, Helen. *The Mixed Blessing.* 2d ed. New York: Popular Library, 1976.

———— *The Rich and the Righteous.* 2d ed. New York: Popular Library, 1977.

———— *Sisters and Strangers.* 2d ed. New York: Popular Library, 1978.

Virga, Vincent. *Gaywick.* New York: Avon Books, 1980.

Walpole, Horace. *The Castle of Otronto.* In *Three Gothic Novels.* Edited by E. F. Bleiler. New York: Dover Publications, 1966.

Wandle, Jennie Taylor. *The Art of Letter-Writing.* New York: A. L. Burt, 1889.

Warner, Lucille S. *Love Comes to Anne.* New York: Scholastic Book Services, Wildfire series, 1979.

White, Jude Gilliam [Devereaux, Jude]. *Highland Velvet.* New York: Pocket Books, 1982.

Whitney, Phyllis A. *The Golden Unicorn.* New York: Doubleday, 1976.

Wilde, Oscar. *The Importance of Being Earnest: a Trivial Comedy for Serious People by the Author of Lady Windermere's Fan.* London: Leonard Smithers and Company, 1898.

Winsor, Kathleen. *Forever Amber.* New York: Macmillan Publishing Co., 1944.

Winspear, Violet. *The Awakening of Alice.* 2d ed. Toronto: Harlequin Books, Presents series, 1978.

———— *Bride of Lucifer.* 2d ed. Toronto: Harlequin Books, Presents series, 1973.

———— *Lucifer's Angel.* 3d ed. Toronto: Harlequin Books, Collection series, 1976.

———— *Palace of the Pomegranate.* 2d ed. Toronto: Harlequin Books, Presents series, 1975.

———— *Satan Took a Bride.* 2d ed. Toronto: Harlequin Books, Presents series, 1976.

Wise, Robert, dir. *The Sound of Music.* With Julie Andrews and Christopher Plummer. Twentieth Century-Fox, 1965.

Woodiwiss, Kathleen E. *Ashes in the Wind.* New York: Avon Books, 1979.

———— *The Flame and the Flower.* New York: Avon Books, 1972.

Index